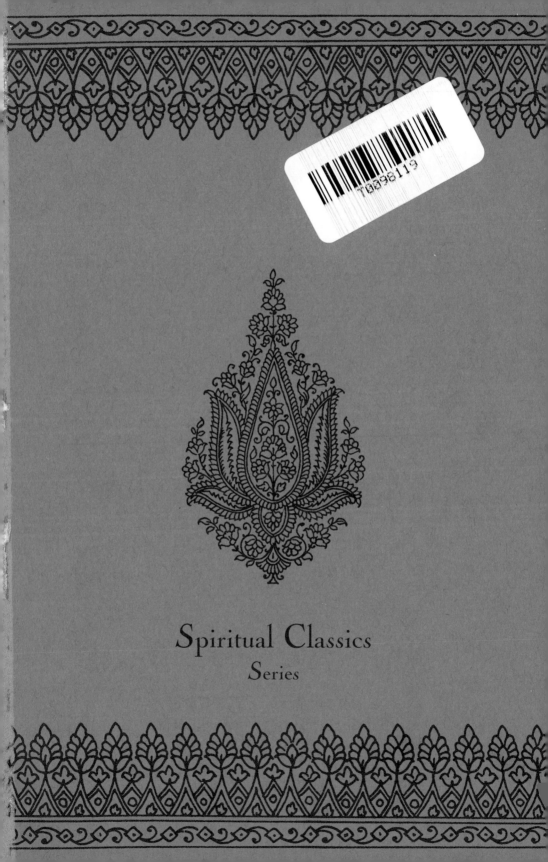

Spiritual Classics

Series

About This Book

"[This book] gives first person narrative to the life of the Dakota, as if you had just been there. Eastman's voice is unfettered by the bias of 'hindsight' or values laden from other times or faiths. This work is a gift of major proportion, to a world in need of gifts, especially those spiritual.... We are grateful for the thoughtful selections from Ohiyesa's work."

—**Janine Pease**, founding president of the Little Big Horn College, and past president of the American Indian Higher Education Consortium

"Michael Fitzgerald has captured the essence of Charles Eastman's writings, focusing on selections from his four best books.... Eastman's words provide his important views regarding Indian and white relations."

—**Prof. Raymond Wilson**, Fort Hays State University

"*The Essential Charles Eastman* is the only modern collection of Eastman's most important writings, and Fitzgerald edited it with a careful attention to the complex deployments Eastman makes of his various identities as well as a sympathetic ear to Eastman's voice, aspirations, and frustrations."

—**Prof. Stephen Brandon**, University of New Mexico

"Michael Fitzgerald's choices represent the pinnacle of Eastman's intent to enlighten and harmonize the disparate elements of these two diametrically opposed, yet convergent cultures: Native America and post-Colonial Civilization. I sincerely recommend *The Essential Charles Eastman* for any educator or interdisciplinary course in which critical comprehension of pan-historic and multi-cultural ideology is vital."

—**Prof. Gerald Musinsky**, Temple University

World Wisdom
The Library of Perennial Philosophy

The Library of Perennial Philosophy is dedicated to the exposition of the timeless Truth underlying the diverse religions. This Truth, often referred to as the *Sophia Perennis*—or Perennial Wisdom—finds its expression in the revealed Scriptures as well as the writings of the great sages and the artistic creations of the traditional worlds.

The Essential Charles Eastman (Ohiyesa): Light on the Indian World appears as one of our selections in the Spiritual Classics series.

Spiritual Classics Series

This series includes seminal, but often neglected, works of unique spiritual insight from leading religious authors of both the East and West. Ranging from books composed in ancient India to forgotten jewels of our time, these important classics feature new introductions which place them in the perennialist context.

The Essential Charles Eastman (Ohiyesa)

Light on the Indian World

Edited by
Michael Oren Fitzgerald

Foreword by
Raymond Wilson

Introduction by
Janine Pease

World Wisdom

The Essential Charles Eastman (Ohiyesa):
Light on the Indian World
© 2007 World Wisdom, Inc.

Library of Congress Cataloging-in-Publication Data

Eastman, Charles Alexander, 1858-1939.
  The essential Charles Eastman (Ohiyesa) : light on the Indian world /
edited by Michael Oren Fitzgerald ; foreword by Raymond Wilson ; intro-
duction by Janine Pease.
     p. cm. – (Sacred worlds series)
  Includes bibliographical references and index.
  ISBN-13: 978-1-933316-33-8 (pbk. : alk. paper)
  ISBN-10: 1-933316-33-0 (pbk. : alk. paper) 1. Indians of North America-
-Religion. 2. Santee Indians–Religion. 3. Indians of North America–
Social life and customs. 4. Santee Indians–Social life and customs. 5.
Indian mythology. 6. Santee mythology. 7. Eastman, Charles Alexander,
1858-1939. I. Fitzgerald, Michael Oren, 1949- II. Title.
  E98.R3E147 2007
  299'.7852–dc22

                                                          2006100068

Printed on acid-free paper in Canada

For information address World Wisdom, Inc.
P.O. Box 2682, Bloomington, Indiana 47402-2682

www.worldwisdom.com

This book is dedicated to all American Indian people.

All royalties from this book will be used to
support the traditional religion
of Plains Indian tribes
or to purchase copies of this book
for distribution to American Indian readers.

Table of Contents

Foreword

Nearly seventy years have passed since the death of Dr. Charles A. Eastman (Ohiyesa) in Detroit, Michigan in 1939. Yet Eastman's impact and significance continue to be critically examined in the twenty-first century. As the foremost educated Indian living in the United States at the beginning of the twentieth century, Eastman endured all kinds of pressure. For example, he was the "Poster Child" for assimilationists; he could not practice medicine successfully as a licensed physician, both on and off Indian reservations; he and his non-Indian wife, Elaine Goodale Eastman, had a volatile marriage that ended in a mutually agreed to secret separation; and he failed to publish after he and his wife separated, even though he was working on several manuscripts.

In spite of all these difficulties, Eastman, with the assistance of his wife, produced many significant publications that enabled non-Indians to better understand Indians, identified Indian issues that needed to be addressed, and called for needed reform legislation to improve Indian conditions.

Michael Fitzgerald has captured the essence and significance of much of what Eastman wrote and demanded in this second edition, now entitled, *The Essential Charles Eastman (Ohiyesa): Light on the Indian World*. Indeed, selections from Eastman's two autobiographies, *Indian Boyhood* (1902) and *From the Deep Woods to Civilization* (1916) provide background on Eastman's life—it is unfortunate that Eastman was unable to complete the third installment of his autobiography, which could have provided important information on his life in the 1920s and 1930s, two decades that are rather sparse on

1. See Sargent, Theodore D. and Raymond Wilson, "Elaine Goodale Eastman: Author and Indian Reformer," in *The Human Tradition in America between the Wars, 1920-1945*, ed. Donald W. Whisenhunt, Wilmington, DE: Scholarly Resources, 2002, p. 89-104.

Eastman's activities. *The Soul of the Indian* (1911) and *The Indian Today* (1915) are Eastman's most profound books, the former providing information on Indian religious beliefs and the latter detailing Indian customs, traditions, and conditions.

Eastman was an acculturated Indian, who adopted the essential elements of the dominant culture and, at the same time, retained much of his Indian beliefs. In *The Essential Charles Eastman (Ohiyesa)*, Michael Fitzgerald has definitely supplied valuable information to better understand this complex and significant individual.

Raymond Wilson
Fort Hays University
October, 2006

Preface

Ohiyesa, also known as Charles Alexander Eastman, was the first great American Indian author, publishing eleven books from 1902 until 1918. In his later adult life he was the foremost Indian spokesman of his day and his contribution to our understanding of the American Indian philosophy and religion are so significant that at the 1933 Chicago World's Fair, Ohiyesa was presented a special medal honoring the most distinguished achievements by an American Indian. Ohiyesa said of his work, "My chief object has been, not to entertain, but to present the American Indian in his true character before Americans. . . . Really it was a campaign of education on the Indian and his true place in American history."[1]

A Santee Sioux, Ohiyesa was born in 1858 and lived the traditional nomadic life of the Sioux in Canada and Minnesota until the age of 15, including the complete training to be a hunter-warrior in the tradition of his forefathers. When his father, who Ohiyesa thought had been killed by whites, suddenly reappeared, the young boy was immersed into the dominant civilization of the white race. He eventually received his undergraduate degree from Dartmouth and obtained his medical degree at Boston College before returning to the Pine Ridge Sioux reservation in South Dakota as their government physician (including tending to casualties at the Wounded Knee massacre). He then spent the majority of the remainder of his life working in various ways to help his native people and to promote a better understanding of the American Indian culture and character. He became the first and arguably the only American Indian to be raised until he was a young man in a complete-

1. Eastman, Charles A., *From the Deep Woods to Civilization*, U. of Nebraska Press, Lincoln, 1977.

ly traditional nomadic life, later receive both undergraduate and graduate college degrees and then continue to dedicate his life to the well being of his native peoples.

As the 20th century began, because the American Indians had no native written language, our understanding of their original philosophy and religion was fragmentary and almost exclusively limited to what had been preserved by white men from the stories of a few Indians. Ohiyesa points out that many of those transmissions are of dubious worth, either because the Indian source was questionable or because the white transcriber was inadequate or prejudiced. Ohiyesa's works are therefore the first and one of the most complete explanations of the philosophy and spiritual traditions of the Plains Indians, indeed any American Indian tribe. Ohiyesa provides much of the basis of our knowledge of the cultural ideal and philosophy of the Plains Indian, an ideal and philosophy that are all the more important today to help us preserve our humanity in the face of our increasingly technological society.

Ohiyesa's writings as a whole have four main themes, with his first and primary goal being to present "the soul of the Indian", namely the original philosophy and the essential spiritual tradition of his native people. He said, "I have attempted to paint the religious life of the typical American Indian as it was before he knew the white man. I have long wished to do this, because I cannot find that it has ever been seriously, adequately, and sincerely done."[2]

A second theme is Ohiyesa's own spiritual quest in a hostile world, including the gradual formation and presentation of his personal philosophy as a man torn between two worlds. One world is that of the spiritual principles of his ancestors and their intimate relationship with virgin nature,

2. Eastman, Charles A., *The Soul of the Indian*, U. of Nebraska Press, Lincoln, 1980.

which forever died at Wounded Knee, and the other world is that of a dominant civilization that does not live up to the religious ideal that it espoused. His two worlds include both his life long belief in his native Indian spirituality and his belief in his adopted Christian religion. Regarding his experience when he first went to school in Iowa, he said, "I was now a stranger in a strange country, and deep in a strange life from which I could not retreat. . . . I simply tried silently to fit the new ideas like so many blocks into the pattern of my philosophy."[3] His careful observations of the ideals and realities of the white civilization of his adult life provide a compelling contrast to the traditional Indian teachings of his youth. For example, he concluded, "It is my personal belief, after thirty-five years' experience of it, that there is no such thing as 'Christian Civilization.' I believe that Christianity and modern civilization are opposed and irreconcilable, and that the spirit of Christianity and of our ancient religion is essentially the same."[4]

The reader is left with a clear portrait of both the philosophy of the original American Indian and the subsequent personal philosophy of a spiritual man who cannot escape his place in modern civilization. "I stand before my own people still as an advocate of civilization. Why? First, because there is no chance for our former simple life any more; and second, because I realize that the white man's religion is not responsible for his mistakes. . . . I am an Indian; and while I have learned much from civilization, for which I am grateful, I have never lost my Indian sense of right and justice. I am for development and progress along social and spiritual lines, rather than those of commerce, nationalism, or material effi-

3. Eastman, Charles A., *From the Deep Woods to Civilization*, U. of Nebraska Press, Lincoln, 1977.
4. Eastman, Charles A., *The Soul of the Indian*, U. of Nebraska Press, Lincoln, 1980.

ciency. Nevertheless, so long as I live, I am an American."[5] Ohiyesa's writings can provide important insights for our own journey through an even more fast-paced and technological world than the world at the beginning of the 20th century.

The third theme of his writings is the inevitable discussion of the injustices that Ohiyesa sees in the treatment of his native peoples, both in the violation of their treaty rights and in the debasing of their culture by the whites, together with his assessment of the practical implications of U.S. governmental policy toward the Indians in the early 20th century. The final theme of his books are the children's stories which were told at night around the campfires by the grandparents to the young ones in the traditional method of transmitting the traditions of his people. Ohiyesa learned many of these stories from the old timers as he lived with them during both his youth and in his adult life.

These "Essential Writings of Ohiyesa" have been arranged to focus on the first two of the aforementioned themes, namely the philosophy and spiritual traditions of the American Indian, and Ohiyesa's personal philosophy, including the essential events in his life that illustrate these two themes. We begin with a large part of *The Soul of the Indian* (1911), the most important book setting forth Ohiyesa's vision of the ideal character of the American Indian. Selections from *The Indian Today* (1915) follow because they are also largely focused on the portrayal of this ideal spiritual philosophy. We then turn to selections from his two auto-biographical works, beginning with *Indian Boyhood* (1902), which is the story of his traditional life in the wild from birth until age 15, during which time he was primarily raised by his grandmother and uncle. Selections from *From the Deep Woods to Civilization* (1916) follow, which begins

5. Eastman, Charles A., *From the Deep Woods to Civilization*, U. of Nebraska Press, Lincoln, 1977.

when he is 15 and the father he thought was dead returns to take him into the white man's civilization. This book chronicles Ohiyesa's life as he is thrust into the white culture and continues until the time of the book's publication when he was 58.

The selections from *The Soul of the Indian* clearly establish the spiritual philosophy of the American Indian to which Ohiyesa continued to be faithful during his entire life. The selections from the next three books round out the picture of the American Indian philosophy and spiritual heritage while also illustrating the difficulties of a man torn between two seemingly irreconcilable worlds. Writings have been deleted that deal with the less essential aspects of his life or that are not relevant to Ohiyesa's two primary themes, including those writings that set forth details of the injustices against his native people, that discuss government or bureaucratic policy, that narrate children's campfire stories, or that are redundant to the selected writings. In several instances editorial notes are inserted that summarize deleted material to provide the context for the selected passages. Deletions are indicated in the body of the text.[6]

Ohiyesa's chief criticism of non-Indian writers was that they interpreted the Indian religion, including the meaning of virgin nature to the Indian, "too much in the light of his present-day environment."[7] In another context he wrote, "There is every evidence that God has given him (the original Indian) all the light necessary by which to live in peace and good-will with his brother; and we also know that many

6. For further study, both *The Soul of the Indian* and *From the Deep Wood to Civilization* are currently available from The University of Nebraska Press.
7. Letter of Charles Eastman to Warren K. Moorehead, March 30, 1915, Warren King Moorehead Papers, Box 27, Ohio State Historical Society, Columbus, Ohio.

brilliant civilizations have collapsed in physical and moral decadence. It is for us to avoid their fate if we can."[8] The goal of these selections is therefore to shed "Light on the Indian World" of Ohiyesa's ancestors; it is our hope that the spiritual values thus illumined can help people of today to strengthen their own spiritual lives even while living in a world that is increasingly antagonistic toward all that is sacred.

Michael Oren Fitzgerald
Bloomington, Indiana
July, 2006

8. Eastman, Charles A., *From the Deep Woods to Civilization*, U. of Nebraska Press, Lincoln, 1977.

Introduction

Ohiyesa, Charles Eastman, is a person with an extraordinary mind and heart. In *The Essential Charles Eastman
(Ohyiesa): Light on the Indian World*, he generously shares with
us, and for time immemorial, his Native knowledge from the
times of Native peoples, whose days have long since concluded. Ohiyesa brings perspective to his journeys, observations
and insights that transcend the usual. He crosses the bound-
aries of space, time, and culture. Through this quality of
human communication, Ohiyesa takes the reader into a
dimension seldom obtained in mere print, be it fiction or
autobiography. This book articulates Native thinking from
the trained and schooled Ohiyesa, prepared for scholarship
within the national knowledge of the Santee Sioux, the
Lakota. The Native thinking is instructed, formed and developed through the spiritual and social values of Ohiyesa's tribe
and family, most especially his grandmother. A person of
enormous heart, Ohiyesa shares "the soul of the Indian,"
terms of his own choosing, and while at times he teeters
between the spiritual values of his upbringing and those of
the people that surround him, he demonstrates via his entire
life, enormity of heart.[1] Essentially, it is courage, the warrior
attribute of heart, that took him through years of life and its
formidable challenges—challenges that killed so many of his
people, if not physically, then spiritually.

Ohiyesa is a fully inculcated Santee Sioux of his era, born
in 1858. As an individual Santee Sioux, he has full membership in the culture, its knowledge, beliefs, art, morals, laws,
customs, capabilities and habits.[2] Ohiyesa learned the life

1. Eastman, Charles A., *From the Deep Woods to Civilization*, University
of Nebraska Press: Lincoln NE, 1977.
2. Kroeber, A.L., *Anthropology: Culture Patterns and Processes*,
Harcourt, Brace and World, Inc.: New York, 1963, p. 60.

attributes of the Santee Sioux from his contemporaries, elders, his relatives and the past. While we approach the life of
Ohiyesa through his narratives, we become critically conscious of the "superorganic," or something more than organic, nature of Santee Sioux life in the mid-nineteenth century.
We can acquire a sense of the "soul" of the people among
whom Ohiyesa lived, as he became a member of their society,
and as that society transitioned through times difficult and
daunting.[3] Ohiyesa brings out the qualities of the Santee
Sioux "soul," as it attached the vital actions and behaviors of
Ohiyesa and the kin of his time.

In this regard, the privilege of Ohiyesa's insight is extraordinary. Only unusually knowing individuals can perceive
their own actions and behaviors and reflect upon their attach-
ment to the entire endowment of their culture. Most human
beings carry out their lives in something of an "automatic
pilot" manner, choosing actions and behaviors somewhat
automatically. As an individual, it is obvious that Ohiyesa's
antecedents were intellectual and investigative, as his training
reflects the values and meanings of actions and behaviors.
The narrative demonstrates the process of knowing and the
analysis of information. These represent a scholarly tradition,
a Santee Sioux scholarly tradition. For this insight, we, the
readers are privileged. However, Ohiyesa is not just devoted
to the narratives, he also comments and analyzes the content
of his narratives. As he assumes a position in the greater
American society, Ohiyesa brings his knowledge and insight
to bear on his experiences, the transitions of his Santee Sioux
people, their status in the country, and the impact of their
history.

Acculturation is a window through which we travel with
Ohiyesa. He describes and analyzes the cultural changes that
come about by way of the influence of the greater American

3. Ibid. p. 61.

culture on the Santee Sioux culture, and in a very personal way, on himself. Acculturation pertains to the influencing of cultures, an influence that may be reciprocal or overwhelmingly one-way.[4] The acculturation of the Santee Sioux dealt a devastating blow to the people in general, and for Ohiyesa, his world changed dramatically. Ohiyesa was forced to make major changes during his life, many of which were overwhelming and hardly by choice. Following the Sioux wars in Minnesota, Ohiyesa was brought abruptly into the shock of cultural contact. As an individual, he could have slid into despondency and hopelessness, like many of his tribe's members. He could have been passive or taken up overt resistance. In spite of the crushing historical events that imperiled the Santee Sioux people, Ohiyesa's band and family, and even Ohiyesa, individually, demonstrated a remarkably resilient spirit, a buoyant spirit.

From his Native foundation, the Santee Sioux culture molded Ohiyesa and demanded his full participation. The childhood training he underwent, his education and religious training, coupled with his own initiative, shaped his human capacities and individual peculiarities. As an individual, he was a person of higher than average intelligence and energy. All cultures have alternatives and choices within their features, and this is where Ohiyesa exhibits peculiarities or idiosyncrasies. During his earliest years, his grandmother directed his education, in tandem with a gentle competition with his older brother. Ohiyesa recounts the challenge and his discovery of methods his grandmother used in vivid learning experiences. His training for the warrior life is detailed in its aspects of peer teaching and elder mentors. Ohiyesa gives us the chance to understand the multiple aspects of the Native ways of knowing and learning. In the "Borderland of Spirits," section VI of the "Soul of the Indian," he describes

4. Ibid. p. 233.

"the powers of concentration and abstraction" known amongst his people, and the concept of spirit twins. Doubtless, his grandmother's perceptivity to "sensations in the breast" started his intuitive capacity for matters of the spirit. Ohiyesa is, indeed, perceptive and, as an individual, especially observant and analytical.

His worldview is generously invested throughout the parts of this work by expressing his "people's concept of existence and their view of the universe and its powers."[5] The relationship with the "Great Mystery" is described in hunting, warfare, ceremonies, family and in personal life. Obviously, Ohiyesa benefited from the learning resources of his entire lifetime: the relationships he had with his kin and their teachings by lesson and example, apprenticeships at the side of masters, and the oral history and literature that provided an inheritance of wisdom and knowledge. It must be kept in mind, throughout this treasure of Native knowledge, that reference works on Native Americans were few. Ohiyesa relies solely upon his first hand knowledge for this treatise about the Santee Sioux religion. He terms the religious practices as "individualist," one mapped even in the womb by the mother.[6] "Spiritual comradeship with the animal creation," in Ohiyesa's words, illustrates the Santee Sioux view of "nature, being more alive and filled with spiritual activity than the Western view of nature."[7] We come to understand the power of vision, the role of the sweat lodge, the Sundance and the pipe. Especially poignant is Ohiyesa's portrayal of religion as pervasive in all of life's activities. Life, even in its mundane moments, for Ohiyesa, was essentially religious.

5. Hultkrantz, Ake, *Native Religions of North America: The Power of Visions and Fertility,* Harper Collins Publishers: New York, 1987. p. 21.
6. Op cit., Eastman, *Soul of the Indian,* 1980.
7. Op cit., Hultkrantz, 1987, p. 24.

The *Indian Today: The Past and Future of the First American,* is a work in which Ohiyesa describes the extended family, the men and women, young and old. Economics, childhood for boys and girls, community relations, warfare and horsemanship are illustrated. As this information unfolds, Ohiyesa provides a comprehensive and seamless view of Santee Sioux life. The complexity of American Indian life has been difficult to obtain, as many authors follow the famous person, an historical event or conflict or tell the warrior's story (a man's story). Ohiyesa skillfully combines the comprehensive portrait of his people, in the full context of life in peaceful times and in warfare. History generally portrays American Indians as war-like (stereotypic and misleading at best), and filled with male images divorced from family. In reality, women, children and elders were deeply involved in the entire enterprise of homeland defense. Noted historian Fred Hoxie comments about the "problem of American Indian history" in *Major Problems in American Indian History.* Hoxie says "contemporary historians (late nineteenth century) describe social processes, and the 'people' in this history do not include Indians and blacks."[8] Gratefully, Ohiyesa provides names, relationships and faces to the "people" of the Santee Sioux. Ohiyesa meticulously gives character, quality and vitality to his grandmother, his uncle and brother. Here, in the same work, we have the "people" described alongside the narrative of critically significant historic events, events that Ohiyesa witnessed himself. Here, the "people," the Santee Sioux as a tribe or nation, are portrayed in their complete life and times, not relegated to a footnote or shear demographic speculation.[9]

8. Hoxie, Frederick, "The Problems of Indian History," In *Major Problems of American Indian History,* Editors, Hurtado, Albert L. and Iverson, Peter, D.C. Heath and Company: Lexington, 1994, p. 34-43.
9. Ibid., p. 35.

So many histories of American Indian people squeeze the vitality out of the people; we miss the values, the sense of beauty and honor, the traditions and customs, and the relationships among the family members. Ohiyesa provides relief from this tyranny, from historians' bias that favors the "civilized" and avoids or intentionally excludes the "primitives." Still more problems exist in American Indian history, for it often segregates American Indians (men, women and children) from the national history. This is true for nearly all five hundred tribes or nations; in history books, American Indians seldom even remotely impinge on the national story. Many historical narratives focus on specific personalities that cast one individual in the spotlight—as enemy of the nation. Ironically, the warrior ethic which Ohiyesa details recounts humility of leadership or chieftainship. A single personality focus is culturally inappropriate from the warrior perspective. Further, history often rides the tide of conflict, and paints the clash of cultures or civilization vs. primitives; how snap-shot oriented this portrayal is! American Indian people enter the pages of history contingent upon the presence of Caucasians in conflict—war, as if nothing happens in these thousands of American Indian lives unless the American army or its representatives are there to be the main actors. In this paradigm of American Indian history, the relations among tribes or nations or the intra-tribal events and affairs are eclipsed entirely.[10]

As an individual, Ohiyesa does show the prevailing opinions or biases toward American Indians, from a social science and historical standpoint. As a structure of his writing, he digresses into analysis and takes up what seems like a conversation with the reader, surely as his contemporaries in American society. From our vantage point, it is important to appreciate the vernacular of the day. Ohiyesa chooses the

10. Ibid, p. 39.

terms that were ascribed to Indian people and their lives.
Some of those terms include: primitive, savage, uncivilized, a
primitive race, training to be civilized, and barbarians. The
redemption of this terminology is found in numerous paral-
lel commentaries on "the strange philosophy of the white
man" and in analysis of values. For example, Ohiyesa says, "In
the mad rush for wealth we have too long overlooked the
foundations of our national welfare."[11] The commentaries
and comparisons are written in the context of prevailing
times and its attitudes. Ohiyesa wrote to a general audience
and endeavored to start where his audience begins, with the
times and their general attitudes. For anyone writing about
American Indians, the problem of vernacular, prevailing attitudes and times, and the historic paradigms are major challenges.

The works of Ohiyesa are monumental treasures and
must be appreciated for their singular nature. The chances of
insight into the comprehensive Santee Sioux and plains
Indian life is so slight. Given the crushing events of Ohiyesa's
time, the probability of finding another highly literate, fully
knowledgeable member of Native society as well as American
society like Ohiyesa, is miniscule. Contemporary biographers
and autobiographers do exist, but most are translations by
anthropologists or historians. Ohiyesa gives us direct communication; we have his works—replete with vitality and
meaning. We do not suffer the vagaries of the translation
process or the potentially tinted lens of cross-cultural interpretation. Narratives of American Indian life are nearly
always veiled; Native voices are hushed or scattered, or even
mute. New methods of collecting history include participant
interviews that capture the story from the ground, and obtain
images and voices, in the first person. Ohiyesa interviews him-

11. Op cit., Eastman, "Indian's Gifts to the Nation," *The Indian
Today: The Past and Future of the First American.*

self and we hear his voice; he observes the participants and he illuminates the images through keen and detailed narrative; he narrates the events of major transition along with participant perspectives that include mothers, children, elders and more.

Michael Oren Fitzgerald, the editor, has brought Ohiyesa's works to the readers, and applied his unique insights in doing so. Fitzgerald has heard the poignant narratives of American Indian people, and has lived among the Crow people for extended periods of time since 1970. He has studied American Indian religious tradition on the earth, among the people, in ceremonies and family gatherings. As readers, we are grateful for the thoughtful selections from Ohiyesa's work, and further, thank Fitzgerald for his deep seated appreciation, honor and respect for American Indian culture, its religion, language and lifeways. Fitzgerald's *Yellowtail: Crow Medicine Man and Sundance Chief* is a unique and timely narrative of an extraordinary Crow man and religious leader of our times, Thomas Yellowtail. During the 1980's, Fitzgerald and Yellowtail developed the work in a truly collaborative project. *Yellowtail* is a tribute to both of them— a work of integrity and understanding. Voices and images are authentic, and the portrayal of Yellowtail and his life is comprehensive, well set within the complexity of Crow life in the 20th century. Fitzgerald is a scholar of the world's religions and has devoted extensive study to the Sundance of the Crow. My fortune is to have known both Yellowtail and Fitzgerald, and to have been a member of the Crow Indian community of Montana. Accolades to Michael Fitzgerald for his efforts to, once again, bring the authentic American Indian to the American public, this time through the voice and images of Ohiyesa's life.

Janine Pease
Lodge Grass, MT
July, 2006

Class photo of Eastman at Dartmouth College.

Selections from

The Soul of the Indian
1911

Foreword

"We also have a religion which was given to our forefathers, and has been handed down to us their children. It
teaches us to be thankful, to be united, and to love one another! We never quarrel about religion."

Thus spoke the great Seneca orator, Red Jacket, in his
superb reply to Missionary Cram more than a century ago,
and I have often heard the same thought expressed by my
countrymen.

I have attempted to paint the religious life of the typical
American Indian as it was before he knew the white man. I
have long wished to do this, because I cannot find that it has
ever been seriously, adequately, and sincerely done. The religion of the Indian is the last thing about him that the man of
another race will ever understand.

First, the Indian does not speak of these deep matters so
long as he believes in them, and when he has ceased to
believe he speaks inaccurately and slightingly.

Second, even if he can be induced to speak, the racial and
religious prejudice of the other stands in the way of his sympathetic comprehension.

Third, practically all existing studies on this subject have
been made during the transition period, when the original
beliefs and philosophy of the native American were already
undergoing rapid disintegration.

There are to be found here and there superficial accounts
of strange customs and ceremonies, of which the symbolism
or inner meaning was largely hidden from the observer; and
there has been a great deal of material collected in recent

years which is without value because it is modern and hybrid, inextricably mixed with Biblical legend and Caucasian philosophy. Some of it has even been invented for commercial purposes. Give an Indian who has lost the traditional ways a present, and he will possibly provide you with sacred songs, a mythology, and folklore to order!

My little book does not pretend to be a scientific treatise. It is as true as I can make it to my childhood teaching and ancestral ideals, but from the human, not the ethnological standpoint. I have not cared to pile up more dry bones, but to clothe them with flesh and blood. So much as has been written by strangers of our ancient faith and worship treats it chiefly as matter of curiosity. I should like to emphasize its universal quality, its personal appeal!

The first missionaries, good men imbued with the narrowness of their age, branded us as pagans and devil-worshippers, and demanded of us that we abjure our false gods before bowing the knee at their sacred altar. They even told us that we were eternally lost, unless we adopted a tangible symbol and professed a particular form of their hydra-headed faith.

We of the twentieth century know better! We know that all religious aspiration, all sincere worship, can have but one source and one goal. We know that the God of the lettered and the unlettered, of the Greek and the barbarian, is after all the same God; and, like Peter, we perceive that He is no respecter of persons, but that in every nation he that feareth Him and worketh righteousness is acceptable to Him.

Charles A. Eastman (Ohiyesa)

The Great Mystery

Solitary Worship. The Savage Philosopher. The Dual Mind. Spiritual Gifts versus Material Progress. The Paradox of "Christian Civilization."

The original attitude of the American Indian toward the Eternal, the "Great Mystery" that surrounds and embraces us, was as simple as it was exalted. To him it was the supreme conception, bringing with it the fullest measure of joy and satisfaction possible in this life.

The worship of the "Great Mystery" was silent, solitary, free from all self-seeking. It was silent, because all speech is of necessity feeble and imperfect; therefore the souls of my ancestors ascended to God in wordless adoration. It was solitary, because they believed that He is nearer to us in solitude, and there were no priests authorized to come between a man and his Maker. None might exhort or confess or in any way meddle with the religious experience of another. Among us all men were created sons of God and stood erect, as conscious of their divinity. Our faith might not be formulated in creeds, nor forced upon any who were unwilling to receive it; hence there was no preaching, proselyting, nor persecution, neither were there any scoffers or atheists.

There were no temples or shrines among us save those of nature. Being a natural man, the Indian was intensely poetical. He would deem it sacrilege to build a house for Him who may be met face to face in the mysterious, shadowy aisles of the primeval forest, or on the sunlit bosom of virgin prairies, upon dizzy spires and pinnacles of naked rock, and yonder in the jeweled vault of the night sky! He who enrobes Himself in filmy veils of cloud, there on the rim of the visible world where our Great-Grandfather Sun kindles his evening campfire, He who rides upon the rigorous wind of the north, or breathes forth His spirit upon aromatic southern airs, whose war-canoe is launched upon majestic rivers and inland seas— He needs no lesser cathedral!

That solitary communion with the Unseen which was the highest expression of our religious life is partly described in the word *hambeday*, literally "mysterious feeling," which has been variously translated "fasting" and "dreaming." It may better be interpreted as "consciousness of the divine."

The first *hambeday*, or religious retreat, marked an epoch in the life of the youth, which may be compared to that of confirmation or conversion in Christian experience. Having first prepared himself by means of the purifying sweat lodge, and cast off as far as possible all human fleshly influences, the young man sought out the noblest height, the most commanding summit in all the surrounding region. Knowing that God sets no value upon material things, he took with him no offerings or sacrifices other than symbolic objects, such as paints and tobacco. Wishing to appear before Him in all humility, he wore no clothing save his moccasins and breech-clout. At the solemn hour of sunrise or sunset he took up his position, overlooking the glories of earth and facing the "Great Mystery," and there he remained, naked, erect, silent, and motionless, exposed to the elements and forces of His arming, for a night and a day to two days and nights, but rarely longer. Sometimes he would chant a hymn without words, or offer the ceremonial "filled pipe." In this holy trance or ecstasy the Indian mystic found his highest happiness and the motive power of his existence.

When he returned to the camp, he must remain at a distance until he had again entered the sweat lodge and prepared himself for intercourse with his fellows. Of the vision or sign vouchsafed to him he did not speak, unless it had included some commission which must be publicly fulfilled. Sometimes an old man, standing upon the brink of eternity, might reveal to a chosen few the oracle of his long-past youth.

The native American has been generally despised by his white conquerors for his poverty and simplicity. They forget, perhaps, that his religion forbade the accumulation of wealth and the enjoyment of luxury. To him, as to other single-minded men in every age and race, from Diogenes to the brothers of Saint Francis, from the Montanists to the Shakers, the love of possessions has appeared a snare, and the burdens of a complex society a source of needless peril and temptation. Furthermore, it was the rule of his life to share the fruits of his skill and success with his less fortunate brothers. Thus he kept his spirit free from the clog of pride, cupidity, or envy, and carried out, as he believed, the divine decree—a matter profoundly important to him.

It was not, then, wholly from ignorance or improvidence that he failed to establish permanent towns and to develop a material civilization. To the untutored sage, the concentration of population was the prolific mother of all evils, moral no less than physical. He argued that food is good, while surfeit kills; that love is good, but lust destroys; and not less dreaded than the pestilence following upon crowded and unsanitary dwellings was the loss of spiritual power inseparable from too close contact with one's fellow-men. All who have lived much out of doors know that there is a magnetic and nervous force that accumulates in solitude and that is quickly dissipated life in a crowd; and even his enemies have recognized the fact that for a certain innate power and self-poise, wholly independent of circumstances, the American Indian is unsurpassed among men.

The red man divided mind into two parts,—the spiritual mind and the physical mind. The first is pure spirit, concerned only with the essence of things, and it was this he sought to strengthen by spiritual prayer, during which the body is subdued by fasting and hardship. In this type of prayer there was no beseeching favor or help. All matters of personal or selfish concern, as success in hunting or warfare, relief from sickness, or the sparing of a beloved life, were definitely relegated to the plane of the lower or material mind, and all ceremonies, charms, or incantations designed to secure a benefit or to avert a danger, were recognized as emanating from the physical self.

The rites of this physical worship, again, were wholly symbolic, and the Indian no more worshiped the Sun than the Christian adores the Cross. The Sun and the Earth, by an obvious parable, holding scarcely more of poetic metaphor than of scientific truth, were in his view the parents of all organic life. From the Sun, as the universal father, proceeds the quickening principle in nature, and in the patient and fruitful womb of our mother, the Earth, are hidden embryos of plants and men. Therefore our reverence and love for them was really an imaginative extension of our love for our immediate parents, and with this sentiment of filial piety was joined a willingness to appeal to them, as to a father, for such good gifts as we may desire. This is the material or physical prayer.

The elements and majestic forces in nature, Lightning, Wind, Water, Fire, and Frost, were regarded with awe as spiritual powers, but always secondary and intermediate in character. We believed that the spirit pervades all creation and that every creature possesses a soul in some degree, though not necessarily a soul conscious of itself. The tree, the waterfall, the grizzly bear, each is an embodied Force, and as such an object of reverence.

The Indian loved to come into sympathy and spiritual communion with his brothers of the animal kingdom, whose inarticulate souls had for him something of the sinless purity that we attribute to the innocent and irresponsible child. He had faith in their instincts, as in a mysterious wisdom given from above; and while he humbly accepted the supposedly voluntary sacrifice of their bodies to preserve his own, he paid homage to their spirits in prescribed prayers and offerings.

In every religion there is an element of the supernatural, varying with the influence of pure reason over its devotees. The Indian was a logical and clear thinker upon matters within the scope of his understanding, but he had not yet charted the vast field of nature or expressed her wonders in terms of science. With his limited knowledge of cause and effect, he saw miracles on every hand,—the miracle of life in seed and egg, the miracle of death in lightning flash and in the swelling deep! Nothing of the marvelous could astonish him; as that a beast should speak, or the sun stand still. The virgin birth would appear scarcely more miraculous than is the birth of every child that comes into the world, or the miracle of the loaves and fishes excite more wonder than the harvest that springs from a single ear of corn.

Who may condemn his superstition? Surely not the devout Catholic even Protestant missionary, who teaches Bible miracles as literal fact! The logical man must either deny all miracles or none, and our American Indian myths and hero stories are perhaps, in themselves, quite as credible as those of the Hebrews of old. If we are of the spiritual type of mind, that sees in natural law a majesty and grandeur far more impressive than any solitary infraction of it could possibly be, let us not forget that, after all, science has not explained everything. We have still to face the ultimate miracle,—the origin and principle of life! Here is the supreme mystery that is the essence of worship, without which there can be no religion, and in the presence of this mystery our attitude cannot be very unlike that of the natural philosopher, who beholds with awe the Divine in all creation.

It is simple truth that the Indian did not, so long as his native philosophy held sway over his mind, either envy or desire to imitate the splendid achievements of the white man. In his own thought he rose superior to them! He scorned them, even as a lofty spirit absorbed in its stern task rejects the soft beds, the luxurious food, the pleasure-worshiping dalliance of a rich neighbor. It was clear to him that virtue and happiness are independent of these things, if not incompatible with them.

There was undoubtedly much in primitive Christianity to appeal to this man, and Jesus' hard sayings to the rich and about the rich would have been entirely comprehensible to him. Yet the religion that is preached in our churches and practiced by our congregations, with its element of display and self-aggrandizement, its active proselytism, and its open contempt of all religions but its own, was for a long time extremely repellent. To his simple mind, the professionalism of the pulpit, the paid exhorter, the moneyed church, was an unspiritual and unedifying thing, and it was not until his spirit was broken and his moral and physical constitution undermined by trade, conquest, and strong drink, that Christian missionaries obtained any real hold upon him. Strange as it may seem, it is true that the proud pagan in his secret soul despised the good men who came to convert and to enlighten him!

Nor were its publicity and its Phariseeism the only elements in the alien religion that offended the red man. To him, it appeared shocking and almost incredible that there were among this people who claimed superiority many irreligious, who did not even pretend to profess the national faith. Not only did they not profess it, but they stooped so low as to insult their God with profane and sacrilegious speech! In our own tongue His name was not spoken aloud, even with utmost reverence, much less lightly or irreverently.

More than this, even in those white men who professed religion we found much inconsistency of conduct. They spoke much of spiritual things, while seeking only the material. They bought and sold everything, labor, personal independence, the love of woman, and even the ministrations of their holy faith! The lust for money, power, and conquest so characteristic of the Anglo-Saxon race did not escape moral condemnation at the hands of his untutored judge, nor did he fail to contrast this conspicuous trait of the dominant race with the spirit of the meek and lowly Jesus.

He might in time come to recognize that the drunkards and licentious among white men, with whom he too frequently came in contact, were condemned by the white man's religion as well, and must not be held to discredit it. But it was not so easy to overlook or to excuse national bad faith. When distinguished emissaries from the Father at Washington, some of them ministers of the gospel and even bishops, came to the Indian nations, and pledged to them in solemn treaty the national honor, with prayer and mention of their God; and when such treaties, so made, were promptly and shamelessly broken, is it strange that the action should arouse not only anger, but contempt? The historians of the white race admit that the Indian was never the first to repudiate his oath.

It is my personal belief, after thirty-five years' experience of it, that there is no such thing as "Christian Civilization." I believe that Christianity and modern civilization are opposed and irreconcilable, and that the spirit of Christianity and of our ancient religion is essentially the same.

The Family Altar

Pre-natal Influence. Early Religious Teaching. The Function of the Aged. Woman, Marriage and the Family. Loyalty, Hospitality, Friendship.

The American Indian was an individualist in religion as in war. He had neither a national army nor an organized church. There was no priest to assume responsibility for another's soul. That is, we believed, the supreme duty of the parent, who only was permitted to claim in some degree the priestly office and function, since it is his creative and protecting power which alone approaches the solemn function of Deity.

The Indian was a religious man from his mother's womb. From the moment of her recognition of the fact of conception to the end of the second year of life, which was the ordinary duration of lactation, it was supposed by us that the mother's spiritual influence counted for most. Her attitude and secret meditations must be such as to instill into the receptive soul of the unborn child the love of the "Great

Mystery" and a sense of brotherhood with all creation. Silence and isolation are the rule of life for the expectant mother. She wanders prayerful in the stillness of great woods, or on the bosom of the untrodden prairie, and to her poetic mind the immanent birth of her child prefigures the advent of a master-man—a hero, or the mother of heroes—a thought conceived in the virgin breast of primeval nature, and dreamed out in a hush that is only broken by the sighing of the pine tree or the thrilling orchestra of a distant waterfall.

And when the day of days in her life dawns—the day in which there is to be a new life, the miracle of whose making has been entrusted to her, she seeks no human aid. She has been trained and prepared in body and mind for this her holiest duty, ever since she can remember. The ordeal is best met alone, where no curious or pitying eyes embarrass her; where all nature says to her spirit: "'Tis love! 'tis love! the fulfilling of life!" When a sacred voice comes to her out of the silence, and a pair of eyes open upon her in the wilderness, she knows with joy that she has borne well her part in the great song of creation!

Presently she returns to the camp, carrying the mysterious, the holy, the dearest bundle! She feels the endearing warmth of it and hears its soft breathing. It is still a part of herself, since both are nourished by the same mouthful, and no look of a lover could be sweeter than its deep, trusting gaze.

She continues her spiritual teaching, at first silently—a mere pointing of the index finger to nature; then in whispered songs, bird-like, at morning and evening. To her and to the child the birds are real people, who live very close to the "Great Mystery"; the murmuring trees breathe His presence; the falling waters chant His praise.

If the child should chance to be fretful, the mother raises her hand. "Hush! hush!" she cautions it tenderly, "the spirits may be disturbed!" She bids it be still and listen to the silver voice of the aspen, or the clashing cymbals of the birch; and at night she points to the heavenly, blazed trail, through nature's galaxy of splendor to nature's God. Silence, love, reverence,—this is the trinity of first lessons; and to these she later adds generosity, courage, and chastity.

In the old days, our mothers were single-eyed to the trust imposed upon them; and as a noted chief of our people was wont to say: "Men may slay one another, but they can never overcome the woman, for in the quietude of her lap lies the child! You may destroy him once and again, but he issues as often from that same gentle lap—a gift of the Great Good to the race, in which man is only an accomplice!"

This wild mother has not only the experience of her mother and grandmother, and the accepted rules of her people for a guide, but she humbly seeks to learn a lesson from ants, bees, spiders, beavers, and badgers. She studies the family life of the birds, so exquisite in its emotional intensity and its patient devotion, until she seems to feel the universal mother-heart beating in her own breast. In due time the child takes of his own accord the attitude of prayer, and speaks reverently of the Powers. He thinks that he is a blood brother to all living creatures, and the storm wind is to him a messenger of the "Great Mystery."

At the age of about eight years, if he is a boy, she turns him over to his father for more Spartan training. If a girl, she is from this time much under the guardianship of her grandmother, who is considered the most dignified protector for the maiden. Indeed, the distinctive work of both grandparents is that of acquainting the youth with the national traditions and beliefs. It is reserved for them to repeat the time-hallowed tales with dignity and authority, so as to lead him into his inheritance in the stored-up wisdom and experience the race. The old are dedicated to the service of the young, as their teachers and advisers, and the young in turn regard them with love and reverence.

Our old age was in some respects the happiest period of life. Advancing years brought with them much freedom, not only from the burden of laborious and dangerous tasks, but from those restrictions of custom and etiquette which were religiously observed by all others. No one who is at all acquainted with the Indian in his home can deny that we are a polite people. As a rule, the warrior who inspired the greatest terror in the hearts of his enemies was a man of the most exemplary gentleness, and almost feminine refinement, among his family and friends. A soft, low voice was considered an excellent thing in man, as well as in woman! Indeed, the enforced intimacy of tent life would soon become intolerable, were it not for these instinctive reserves and delicacies, this unfailing respect for the established place and possessions of every other member of the family circle, this habitual quiet, order, and decorum.

Our people, though capable of strong and durable feeling, were not demonstrative in their affection at any time, least of all in the presence of guests or strangers. Only to the aged, who have journeyed far, and are in a manner exempt from ordinary rules, are permitted some playful familiarities with children and grandchildren, some plain speaking, even to harshness and objurgation, from which the others must rigidly refrain. In short, the old men and women are privileged to say what they please and how they please, without contradiction, while the hardships and bodily infirmities that of necessity fall to their lot are softened so far as may be by universal consideration and attention.

There was no religious ceremony connected with marriage among us, while on the other hand the relation between man and woman was regarded as in itself mysterious and holy. It appears that where marriage is solemnized by the church and blessed by the priest, it may at the same time be surrounded with customs and ideas of a frivolous, superficial, and even prurient character. We believed that two who love should be united in secret, before the public acknowledgment of their union, and should taste their apotheosis with nature. The betrothal might or might not be discussed and approved by the parents, but in either case it was customary for the young pair to disappear into the wilderness, there to pass some days or weeks in perfect seclusion and dual solitude, afterward returning to the village as man and wife. An exchange of presents and entertainments between the two families usually followed, but the nuptial blessing was given by the High Priest of God, the most reverend and holy Nature.

The family was not only the social unit, but also the unit of government clan is nothing more than a larger family, with its patriarchal chief as the natural head, and the union of several clans by inter-marriage and voluntary connection constitutes the tribe. The very name of our tribe, Dakota, means Allied People. The remoter degrees of kinship were fully recognized, and that not as a matter of form only: first cousins were known as brothers and sisters; the name of "cousin" constituted binding claim, and our rigid morality forbade marriage between cousins in any known degree, or in other words within the clan.

The household proper consisted of a man with one or more wives and their children, all of whom dwelt amicably together, often under one roof, although some men of rank and position provided a separate lodge for each wife. There were, indeed, few plural marriages except among the older and leading men, and plural wives were usually, though not necessarily, sisters. A marriage might honorably be dissolved for cause, but there was very little infidelity or immorality, either open or secret.

It has been said that the position of woman is the test of civilization, and that of our women was secure. In them was vested our standard of morals and the purity of our blood. The wife did not take the name of her husband nor enter his clan, and the children belonged to the clan of the mother. All of the family property was held by her, descent was traced in the maternal line, and the honor of the house was in her hands. Modesty was her chief adornment; hence the younger women were usually silent and retiring: but a woman who had attained to ripeness of years and wisdom, or who had displayed notable courage in some emergency, was sometimes invited to a seat in the council.

Thus she ruled undisputed within her own domain, and was to us a tower of moral and spiritual strength, until the coming of the border white man, the soldier and trader, who with strong drink overthrew the honor of the man, and through his power over a worthless husband purchased the virtue of his wife or his daughter. When she fell, the whole race fell with her.

Before this calamity came upon us, you could not find anywhere a happier home than that created by the Indian woman. There was nothing of the artificial about her person, and very little disingenuousness in her character. Her early and consistent training, the definiteness of her vocation, and, above all, her profoundly religious attitude gave her a strength and poise that could not be overcome by any ordinary misfortune.

Indian names were either characteristic nicknames given in a playful spirit, deed names, birth names, or such as have a religious and symbolic meaning . It has been said that when a child is born, some accident or unusual appearance determines his name. This is sometimes the case, but is not the rule. A man of forcible character, with a fine war record, usually bears the name of the buffalo or bear, lightning or some dread natural force. Another of more peaceful nature may be called Swift Bird or Blue Sky. A woman's name usually suggested something about the home, often with the adjective "pretty" or "good," and a feminine termination. Names of any dignity or importance must be conferred by the old men, and especially so if they have any spiritual significance; as Sacred Cloud, Mysterious Night, Spirit Woman, and the like. Such a name was sometimes borne by three generations, but each individual must prove that he is worthy of it.

In the life of the Indian there was only one inevitable duty,—the duty of prayer—the daily recognition of the Unseen and Eternal. His daily devotions were more necessary to him than daily food. He wakes at daybreak, puts on his moccasins and steps down to the water's edge. Here he throws handfuls of clear, cold water into his face, or plunges in bodily. After the bath, he stands erect before the advancing dawn, facing the sun as it dances upon the horizon, and offers his unspoken orison. His mate may precede or follow him in his devotions, but never accompanies him. Each soul must meet the morning sun, the new, sweet earth, and the Great Silence alone!

Whenever, in the course of the daily hunt, the red hunter comes upon a scene that is strikingly beautiful and sublime— a black thunder-cloud with the rainbow's glowing arch above the mountain; a white waterfall in the heart of a green gorge; a vast prairie tinged with the blood-red of sunset—he pauses for an instant in the attitude of worship. He sees no need for setting apart one day in seven as a holy day, since to him all days are God's.

Every act of his life is, in a very real sense, a religious act. He recognizes the spirit in all creation, and believes that he draws from it spiritual power. His respect for the immortal part of the animal, his brother, often leads him so far as to lay out the body of his game in state and decorate the head with symbolic paint or feathers. Then he stands before it in the prayer attitude, holding up the filled pipe, in token that he has freed with honor the spirit of his brother, whose body his need compelled him to take to sustain his own life.

When food is taken, the woman murmurs a "grace" as she lowers the kettle; an act so softly and unobtrusively per- formed that one who does not know the custom usually fails to catch the whisper: "Spirit, partake!" As her husband receives the bowl or plate, he likewise murmurs his invoca- tion to the spirit. When he becomes an old man, he loves to make a notable effort to prove his gratitude. He cuts off the choicest morsel of the meat and casts it into the fire—the purest and most ethereal element.

The hospitality of the wigwam is only limited by the institution of war. Yet, if an enemy should honor us with a call, his trust will not be misplaced, and he will go away convinced that he has met with a royal host! Our honor is the guarantee for his safety, so long as he is within the camp.

Friendship is held to be the severest test of character. It is easy, we think, to be loyal to family and clan, whose blood is in our own veins. Love between man and woman is founded on the mating instinct and is not free from desire and self-seeking. But to have a friend, and to be true under any and all trials, is the mark of a man!

The highest type of friendship is the relation of "brother-friend" or "life-and-death friend." This bond is between man and man, is usually formed in early youth, and can only be broken by death. It is the essence of comradeship and fraternal love, without thought of pleasure or gain, but rather for moral support and inspiration. Each is vowed to die for the other, if need be, and nothing denied the brother-friend, but neither is anything required that is not in accord with the highest conceptions of the Indian mind.

Ceremonial and Symbolic Worship

Modern Perversions of Early Religious Rites. The Sun Dance. Totems and Charms. The Sweat lodge and the Ceremonial of the Pipe.

The public religious rites of the Plains Indians are few, and in large part of modern origin, belonging properly to the so-called "transition period." That period must be held to begin with the first insidious effect upon their manners and customs of contact with the dominant race, and many of the tribes were so influenced long before they ceased to lead the nomadic life.

The fur-traders, the "Black Robe" priests, the military, and finally the Protestant missionaries, were the men who began the disintegration of the Indian nations and the overthrow of their religion, seventy-five to a hundred years before they were forced to enter upon reservation life. We have no authentic study of them until well along in the transition period, when whiskey and trade had already debauched their native ideals.

During the era of reconstruction they modified their customs and beliefs continually, creating a singular admixture of Christian with pagan superstitions, and an addition to the old folk-lore of disguised Bible stories under an Indian aspect. Even their music shows the influence of the Catholic chants. Most of the material collected by modern observers is necessarily of this promiscuous character.

In the old days, when a Sioux warrior found himself in the very jaws of destruction, he might offer a prayer to his father, the Sun, to prolong his life. If rescued from imminent danger, he must acknowledge the divine favor by making a Sun Dance, according to the vow embraced in his prayer, in which he declared that he did not fear torture or death, but asked life only for the sake of those who loved him. Thus the physical ordeal was the fulfillment of a vow, and a sort of atonement for what might otherwise appear to be reprehensible weakness in the face of death. It was in the nature of confession and thank-offering to the "Great Mystery," through the physical parent, the Sun, and did not embrace a prayer for future favors.

The ceremonies usually took place from six months to a year after the making of the vow, in order to admit of suitable preparation; always in midsummer and before a large and imposing gathering. They naturally included the making of a feast, and the giving away of much savage wealth in honor of the occasion, although these were no essential part of the religious rite.

When the day came to procure the pole, it was brought in by a party of warriors, headed by some man of distinction. The tree selected was six to eight inches in diameter at the base, and twenty to twenty-five feet high. It was chosen and felled with some solemnity, including the ceremony of the "filled pipe," and was carried in the fashion of a litter, symbolizing the body of the man who made the dance. A solitary teepee was pitched on a level spot at some distance from the village the pole raised near at hand with the same ceremony, in the centre a circular enclosure of fresh-cut.

Meanwhile, one of the most noted of our old men had carved out of rawhide, or later of wood, two figures, usually those of a man and a buffalo. Sometimes the figure of a bird, supposed to represent the Thunder, was substituted for the buffalo. It was customary to paint the man red and the animal black, and each was suspended from one end of the cross-bar which was securely tied some two feet from the top of the pole. I have never been able to determine that this cross had any significance; it was probably nothing more than a dramatic coincidence that surmounted the Sun-Dance pole with the symbol of Christianity.

The paint indicated that the man who was about to give thanks publicly had been potentially dead, but was allowed to live by the mysterious favor and interference of the Giver of Life. The buffalo hung opposite the image of his own body in death, because it was the support of his physical self, and a leading figure in legendary lore. Following the same line of thought, when he emerged from the solitary lodge of preparation, and approached the pole to dance, nude save for his breech-clout and moccasins, his hair loosened and daubed with clay, he must drag after him a buffalo skull, representing the grave from which he had escaped.

The dancer was cut or scarified on the chest, sufficient to draw blood and cause pain, the natural accompaniments of his figurative death. He took his position opposite the singers, facing the pole, and dragging the skull by leather thongs which were merely fastened about his shoulders. During a later period, incisions were made in the breast or back, sometimes both, through which wooden skewers were drawn, and secured by lariats to the pole or to the skulls. Thus he danced without intermission for a day and a night, or even longer, ever gazing at the sun in the daytime, and blowing from time to time a sacred whistle made from the bone of a goose's wing. . . .

There is no doubt that the Indian held medicine close to spiritual things, but in this also he has been much misunderstood; in fact everything that he held sacred is indiscriminately called "medicine," in the sense of mystery or magic. As a doctor he was originally very adroit and often successful. He employed only healing bark, roots, and leaves with whose properties he was familiar, using them in the form of a distillation or tea and always singly. The stomach or internal bath was a valuable discovery of his, and the sweat lodge or Turkish bath was in general use. He could set a broken bone with fair success, but never practiced surgery in any form. In addition to all this, the medicine-man possessed much personal magnetism and authority, and in his treatment often sought to reestablish the equilibrium of the patient through mental or spiritual influences—a sort of primitive psychotherapy.

The Sioux word for the healing art is "*wah-pee-yah*," which literally means readjusting or making anew. "*Pay-jee-hoo-tah*," literally root, means medicine, and "*wakan*" signifies spirit or mystery. Thus the three ideas, while sometimes associated, were carefully distinguished.

It is important to remember that in the old days the "medicine-man" received no payment for his services, which were of the nature of an honorable function or office. When the idea of payment and barter was introduced among us, and valuable presents or fees began to be demanded for treating the sick, the ensuing greed and rivalry led to many demoralizing practices, and in time to the rise of the modern "conjurer," who is generally a fraud and trickster of the grossest kind. It is fortunate that his day is practically over.

Ever seeking to establish spiritual comradeship with the animal creation, the Indian adopted this or that animal as his "totem," the emblematic device of his society, family, or clan. It is probable that the creature chosen was the traditional ancestress, as we are told that the First Man had many wives among the animal people. The sacred beast, bird, or reptile, represented by its stuffed skin, or by a rude painting, was treated with reverence and carried into battle to insure the guardianship of the spirits. The symbolic attribute of beaver, bear, or tortoise, such as wisdom, cunning, courage, and the like, was supposed to be mysteriously conferred upon the wearer of the badge. The totem or charm used in medicine was ordinarily that of the medicine lodge to which the practitioner belonged, though there were some great men who boasted a special revelation.

There are two ceremonial usages which, so far as I have been able to ascertain, were universal among American Indians, and apparently fundamental. These have already been referred to as the "*eneepee*," or sweat lodge, and the "*chan-du-hupah-za-pee*," or ceremonial of the pipe. In our Siouan legends and traditions these two are preeminent, as handed down from the most ancient time and persisting to the last.

In our Creation myth or story of the First Man, the sweat lodge was the magic used by The-one-who-was-First-Created, to give life to the dead bones of his younger brother, who had been slain by the monsters of the deep. Upon the shore of the Great Water he dug two round holes, over one of which he built a low enclosure of fragrant cedar boughs, and here he gathered together the bones of his brother. In the other pit he made a fire and heated four round stones, which he rolled one by one into the lodge of boughs. Having closed every aperture save one, he sang a mystic chant while he thrust in his arm and sprinkled water upon the stones with a bunch of sage. Immediately steam arose, and as the legend says, "there was an appearance of life." A second time he sprinkled water, and the dry bones rattled together. The third time he seemed to hear soft singing from within the lodge; and the fourth time a voice exclaimed: "Brother, let me out!" (It should be noted that the number four is the magic or sacred number of the Indian.)

This story gives the traditional origin of the "*eneepee*," which has ever since been deemed essential to the Indian's effort to purify and recreate his spirit. It is used both by the doctor and by his patient. Every man must enter the cleansing bath and take the cold plunge which follows, when preparing for any spiritual crisis, for possible death, or imminent danger.

Not only the "*eneepee*" itself, but everything used in connection with the mysterious event, the aromatic cedar and sage, the water, and especially the water-worn boulders, are regarded as sacred, or at the least adapted to a spiritual use. For the rock we have a special reverent name—"*Tunkan*," a contraction of the Sioux word for Grandfather.

The natural boulder enters into many of our solemn ceremonials, such as the "Rain Dance," and the "Feast of Virgins." The lone hunter and warrior reverently holds up his filled pipe to "*Tunkan*," in solitary commemoration of a miracle which to him is as authentic and holy as the raising of Lazarus to the devout Christian.

There is a legend that the First Man fell sick, and was taught by his Elder Brother the ceremonial use of the pipe, in a prayer to the spirits for ease and relief. This simple ceremony is the commonest daily expression of thanks or "grace," as well as an oath of loyalty and good faith when the warrior goes forth upon some perilous enterprise, and it enters even into his "*hambeday*," or solitary prayer, ascending as a rising vapor or incense to the Father of Spirits.

In all the war ceremonies and in medicine a special pipe is used, but at home or on the hunt the warrior employs his own. The pulverized weed is mixed with aromatic bark of the red willow, and pressed lightly into the bowl of the long stone pipe. The worshipper lights it gravely and takes a whiff or two; then, standing erect, he holds it silently toward the Sun, our father, and toward the earth, our mother. There are modern variations, as holding the pipe to the Four Winds, the Fire, Water, Rock, and other elements or objects of reverence.

There are many religious festivals which are local and special in character, embodying a prayer for success in hunting or warfare, or for rain and bountiful harvests, but these two are the sacraments of our religion. For baptism we substitute the "*eneepee*," the purification by vapor, and in our holy communion we partake of the soothing incense of tobacco in the stead of bread and wine.

Barbarism and the Moral Code

Silence the Corner-Stone of Character. Basic Ideas of Morality. "Give All or Nothing!" Rules of Honorable Warfare. An Indian Conception of Courage.

Long before I ever heard of Christ, or saw a white man, I had learned from an untutored woman the essence of morality. With the help of dear Nature herself, she taught me things simple but of mighty import. I knew God. I perceived what goodness is. I saw and loved what is really beautiful. Civilization has not taught me anything better!

As a child, I understood how to give; I have forgotten that grace since I became civilized. I lived the natural life, whereas I now live the artificial. Any pretty pebble was valuable to me then; every growing tree an object of reverence. Now I worship with the white man before a painted landscape whose value is estimated in dollars! Thus the Indian is reconstructed, as the natural rocks are ground to powder, and made into artificial blocks which may be built into the walls of modern society.

The first American mingled with his pride a singular humility. Spiritual arrogance was foreign to his nature and teaching. He never claimed that the power of articulate speech was proof of superiority over the dumb creation; on the other hand, it is to him a perilous gift. He believed profoundly in silence—the sign of a perfect equilibrium. Silence is the absolute poise or balance of body, mind, and spirit. The man who preserves his selfhood ever calm and unshaken by the storms of existence—not a leaf, as it were, astir on the tree; not a ripple upon the surface of shining pool—his, in the mind of the unlettered sage, is the ideal attitude and conduct of life.

If you ask him: "What is silence?" he will answer: "It is the Great Mystery!" "The holy silence is His voice!" If you ask: "What are the fruits of silence?" he will say: "They are self-control, true courage or endurance, patience, dignity, and reverence. Silence is the cornerstone of character."

"Guard your tongue in youth," said the old chief, Wabashaw, "and in age you may mature a thought that will be of service to your people!"

The moment that man conceived of a perfect body, supple, symmetrical, graceful, and enduring—in that moment he had laid the foundation of a moral life! No man can hope to maintain such a temple of the spirit beyond the period of adolescence, unless he is able to curb his indulgence in the pleasures of the senses. Upon this truth the Indian built a rigid system of physical training, a social and moral code that was the law of his life.

There was aroused in him as a child a high ideal of manly strength and beauty, the attainment of which must depend upon strict temperance in eating and in the sexual relation, together with severe and persistent exercise. He desired to be a worthy link in the generations, and that he might not destroy by his weakness that vigor and purity of blood which had been achieved at the cost of much self-denial by a long line of ancestors.

He was required to fast from time to time for short periods, and to work off his superfluous energy by means of hard running, swimming, and the sweat lodge. The bodily fatigue thus induced, especially when coupled with a reduced diet, is a reliable cure for undue sexual desires.

Personal modesty was early cultivated as a safeguard, together with a strong self-respect and pride of family and race. This was accomplished in part by keeping the child ever before the public eye, from his birth onward. His entrance into the world, especially in the case of the first-born, was often publicly announced by the herald, accompanied by a distribution of presents to the old and needy. The same thing occurred when he took his first step, when his ears were pierced, and when he shot his first game, so that his childish exploits and progress were known to the whole clan as to a larger family, and he grew into manhood with the saving sense of a reputation to sustain.

The youth was encouraged to enlist early in the public service, and to develop a wholesome ambition for the honors of a leader and feast maker, which can never be his unless he is truthful and generous, as well as brave, and ever mindful of his personal chastity and honor. There were many ceremonial customs which had a distinct moral influence; the woman was rigidly secluded at certain periods, and the young husband was forbidden to approach his own wife when preparing for war or for any religious event. The public or tribal position of the Indian is entirely dependent on his private virtue, and he is never permitted to forget that he does not live to himself alone, but to his tribe and his clan. Thus habits of perfect self-control were early established, and there were no unnatural conditions or complex temptations to beset him until he was met and overthrown by a stronger race.

To keep the young men and young women strictly to their honor, there were observed among us, within my own recollection, certain annual ceremonies of a semi-religious nature. One of the most impressive of these was the sacred "Feast of Virgins," which, when given for the first time, was equivalent to the public announcement of a young girl's arrival at a marriageable age. The herald, making the rounds of the teepee village, would publish the feast something after this fashion:

"Pretty Weasel-woman, the daughter Brave Bear, will kindle her first maidens' fire to-morrow! All ye who have never yielded to the pleading man, who have not destroyed your innocency, you alone are invited to proclaim anew before the Sun and the Earth, before your companions and in the sight of the Great Mystery, the chastity and purity of your maidenhood. Come ye, all who have not known man!"

The whole village was at once aroused to the interest of the coming event, which was considered next to the Sun Dance and the Grand Medicine Dance in public importance. It always took place in midsummer, when a number of different clans were gathered together for the summer festivities, and was held in the centre of the great circular encampment.

Here two circles were described, one within the other, about a rudely heart-shaped rock which was touched with red paint, and upon either side of the rock there were thrust into the ground a knife and two arrows. The inner circle was for the maidens, and the outer one for their grandmothers or chaperones, who were supposed to have passed the climacteric. Upon the outskirts of the feast there was a great public gathering, in which order was kept by certain warriors of highest reputation. Any man among the spectators might approach and challenge any young woman whom he knew to be unworthy; if the accuser failed to prove his charge, the warriors were accustomed to punish him severely.

Each girl in turn approached the sacred rock and laid her hand upon it with all solemnity. This was her religious declaration of her virginity, her vow to remain pure until her marriage. If she should ever violate the maidens' oath, then welcome that keen knife and those sharp arrows!

25

Our maidens were ambitious to attend a number of these feasts before marriage, and it sometimes happened that a girl was compelled to give one, on account of gossip about her conduct. Then it was in the nature of a challenge to the scandal-mongers to prove their words! A similar feast was sometimes made by the young men, for whom the rules were even more strict, since no young man might attend this feast who had so much as spoken of love to a maiden. It was considered a high honor among us to have won some distinction in war and the chase, and above all to have been invited to a seat in the council, before one had spoken to any girl save his own sister.

It was our belief that the love of possessions is a weakness to be overcome. Its appeal is to the material part, and if allowed its way it will in time disturb the spiritual balance of the man. Therefore the child must early learn the beauty of generosity. He is taught to give what he prizes most, and that he may taste the happiness of giving, he is made at an early age the family almoner. If a child is inclined to be grasping, or to cling to any of his little possessions, legends are related to him, telling of the contempt and disgrace falling upon the ungenerous and mean man.

Public giving is a part of every important ceremony. It properly belongs to the celebration of birth, marriage, and death, and is observed whenever it is desired to do special honor to any person or event. Upon such occasions it is common to give to the point of utter impoverishment. The Indian in his simplicity literally gives away all that he has, to relatives, to guests of another tribe or clan, but above all to the poor and the aged, from whom he can hope for no return. Finally, the gift to the "Great Mystery," the religious offering, may be of little value in itself, but to the giver's own thought it should carry the meaning and reward of true sacrifice.

Orphans and the aged are invariably cared for, not only by their next of kin, but by the whole clan. It is the loving parent's pride to have his daughters visit the unfortunate and the helpless, carry them food, comb their hair, and mend their garments. The name "Wenonah," bestowed upon the eldest daughter, distinctly implies all this, and a girl who failed in her charitable duties was held to be unworthy of the name.

The man who is a skillful hunter, and whose wife is alive to her opportunities makes many feasts, to which he is careful to invite the older men of his clan, recognizing that they have outlived their period of greatest activity, and now love nothing so well as to eat in good company, and to live over the past. The old men, for their part, do their best to requite his liberality with a little speech, in which they are apt to relate the brave and generous deeds of their host's ancestors, finally congratulating him upon being a worthy successor of an honorable line. Thus his reputation is won as a hunter and a feast-maker, and almost as famous in his way as the great warrior is he who has a recognized name and standing as a "man of peace."

The true Indian sets no price upon either his property or his labor. His generosity is only limited by his strength and ability. He regards it as an honor to be selected for a difficult or dangerous service, and would think it shame to ask for any reward, saying rather: "Let him whom I serve express his thanks according to his own bringing up and his sense of honor!"

Nevertheless, he recognizes rights in property. To steal from one of his own tribe would be indeed disgrace if discovered, the name of "*Wamanon*," or Thief, is fixed upon him forever as an unalterable. The only exception to the rule is in the case of food, which is always free to the hungry if there is none by to offer it. Other protection than the moral law there could not be in an Indian community, where there were neither locks nor doors, and everything was open and easy of access to all comers.

The property of the enemy is spoil of war, and it is always allowable to confiscate it if possible. However, in the old days there was not much plunder. Before the coming of the white man, there was in fact little temptation or opportunity to despoil the enemy; but in modern times the practice of "stealing horses" from hostile tribes has become common, and is thought far from dishonorable.

Warfare we regarded as an institution—the "Great Mystery"—an organized tournament or trial of courage and skill, with elaborate rules and "counts" for the coveted honor of the eagle feather. It was held to develop the quality of manliness and its motive was chivalric or patriotic, but never the desire for territorial aggrandizement or the overthrow of a brother nation. It was common, in early times, for a battle or skirmish to last all day, with great display of daring and horsemanship with scarcely more killed and wounded than may be carried from the field during a university game of football.

The slayer of a man in battle was expected to mourn for thirty days, blackening his face and loosening his hair according to the custom. He of course considered it no sin to take the life of an enemy, and this ceremonial mourning was a sign of reverence for the departed spirit. The killing in war of noncombatants, such as women and children, is partly explained by the fact that in savage life the woman without husband or protector is in pitiable case, and it was supposed that the spirit of the warrior would be better content if no widow and orphans were left to suffer want, as well as to weep.

A scalp might originally be taken by the leader of the war party only, and at that period no other mutilation was practiced. It was a small lock not more than three inches square, which was carried only during the thirty days' celebration of a victory, and afterward given religious burial. Wanton cruelties and the more barbarous customs of war were greatly intensified with the coming of the white man, who brought with him fiery liquor and deadly weapons, aroused the Indian's worst passions, provoking in him revenge and cupidity, and even offered bounties for the scalps of innocent men, women, and children.

Murder within the tribe was a grave offense, to be atoned for as the council might decree, and it often happened that the slayer was called upon to pay the penalty with his own life. He made no attempt to escape or to evade justice. That the crime was committed in the depths of the forest or at dead of night, witnessed by no human eye, made no difference to his mind. He was thoroughly convinced that all is known to the "Great Mystery," and hence did not hesitate to give himself up, to stand his trial by the old and wise men of the victim's clan. His own family and clan might by no means attempt to excuse or to defend him, but his judges took all the known circumstances into consideration, and if it appeared that he slew in self-defense, or that the provocation was severe, he might be set free after a thirty days' period of mourning in solitude. Otherwise the murdered man's next of kin were authorized to take his life; and if they refrained from doing so, as often happened, he remained an outcast from the clan. A willful murder was a rare occurrence before the days of whiskey and drunken rows, for we were not a violent or a quarrelsome people. . . .

It is said that, in the very early days, lying was a capital offense among us. Believing that the deliberate liar is capable of committing any crime behind the screen of cowardly untruth and double-dealing, the destroyer of mutual confidence was summarily put to death, that the evil might go no further.

Even the worst enemies of the Indian, those who accuse him of treachery, blood-thirstiness, cruelty, and lust, have not denied his courage but in their minds it is a courage that is ignorant, brutal, and fantastic. His own conception of bravery makes of it a high moral virtue, for to him it consists not so much in aggressive self-assertion as in absolute self-control. The truly brave man, we contend, yields neither to fear nor anger, desire nor agony; he is at all times master of himself; his courage rises to the heights of chivalry, patriotism, and real heroism.

"Let neither cold, hunger, nor pain, nor the fear of them, neither the bristling teeth of danger nor the very jaws of death itself, prevent you from doing a good deed," said an old chief to a scout who was about to seek the buffalo in midwinter for the relief of a starving people. This was his childlike conception of courage.

The Unwritten Scriptures

A Living Book. The Sioux Story of Creation. The First Battle.

A missionary once undertook to instruct a group of Indians in the truths of his holy religion. He told them of the creation of the earth in six days, and of the fall of our first parents by eating an apple.

The courteous savages listened attentively, and after thanking him, one related in his turn a very ancient tradition concerning the origin of the maize. But the missionary plainly showed his disgust and disbelief, indignantly saying:— "What I delivered to you were sacred truths, but this that you tell me is mere fable and falsehood!"

"My brother," gravely replied the offended Indian, "it seems that you have not been well grounded in the rules of civility. You saw that we, who practice these rules, believed your stories; why, then, do you refuse to credit ours?"

Every religion has its Holy Book, and ours was a mingling of history, poetry, and prophecy, of precept and folk-lore, even such as the modern reader finds within the covers of his Bible. This Bible of ours was our whole literature, a living Book, sowed as precious seed by our wisest sages, and springing anew in the wondering eyes and upon the innocent lips of little children. Upon its hoary wisdom of proverb and fable, its mystic and legendary lore thus sacredly preserved and transmitted from father to son, was based in large part our customs and philosophy.

Naturally magnanimous and open-minded, the red man prefers to believe that the Spirit of God is not breathed into man alone, but that the whole created universe is a sharer in the immortal perfection of its Maker. His imaginative and poetic mind, like that of the Greek, assigns to every mountain, tree, and spring its spirit, nymph, or divinity either beneficent or mischievous. The heroes and demigods of Indian tradition reflect the characteristic trend of his thought, and his attribution of personality and will to the elements, the sun and stars, and all animate or inanimate nature.

In the Sioux story of creation, the great Mysterious One is not brought directly upon the scene or conceived in anthropomorphic fashion, but remains sublimely in the background. The Sun and the Earth, representing the male and female principles, are the main elements in his creation, the other planets being subsidiary. The enkindling warmth of the Sun entered into the bosom of our mother, the Earth, and forthwith she conceived and brought forth life, both vegetable and animal.

Finally there appeared mysteriously *Ish-na-e-cha-ge*, the "First-Born," a being in the likeness of man, yet more than man, who roamed solitary among the animal people and understood their ways and their language. They beheld him with wonder and awe, for they could do nothing without his knowledge. He had pitched his tent in the centre of the land, and there was no spot impossible for him to penetrate.

At last, like Adam, the "First-Born" of the Sioux became weary of living alone, and formed for himself a companion— not a mate, but a brother—not out of a rib from his side, but from a splinter which he drew from his great toe! This was the Little Boy Man, who was not created full-grown, but as an innocent child, trusting and helpless. His Elder Brother was his teacher throughout every stage of human progress from infancy to manhood, and it is to the rules which he laid down, and his counsels to the Little Boy Man, that we trace many of our most deep-rooted beliefs and most sacred customs.

Foremost among the animal people was *Unk-to-mee*, the Spider, the original trouble-maker, who noted keenly the growth of the boy in wit and ingenuity, and presently advised the animals to make an end of him; "for," said he, "if you do not, some day he will be the master of us all!" But they all loved the Little Boy Man because he was so friendly and so playful. Only the monsters of the deep sea listened, and presently took his life, hiding his body in the bottom of the sea. Nevertheless, by the magic power of the First-Born, the body was recovered and was given life again in the sacred sweat lodge, as described in a former chapter.

Once more our first ancestor roamed happily among the animal people, who were in those days a powerful nation. He learned their ways and their language—for they had a common tongue in those days; learned to sing like the birds, to swim like the fishes, and to climb sure-footed over rocks like the mountain sheep. Notwithstanding that he was their good comrade and did them no harm, *Unk-to-mee* once more sowed dissension among the animals, and messages were sent into all quarters of the earth, sea, and air, that all the tribes might unite to declare war upon the solitary man who was destined to become their master.

After a time the young man discovered the plot, and came home very sorrowful. He loved his animal friends, and was grieved that they should combine against him. Besides, he was naked and unarmed. But his Elder Brother armed him with a bow and flint-headed arrows, a stone war-club and a spear. He likewise tossed a pebble four times into the air, and each time it became a cliff or wall of rock about the teepee.

"Now," said he, "it is time to fight and to assert your supremacy, for it is they who have brought the trouble upon you, and not you upon them!"

Night and day the Little Boy Man remained upon the watch for his enemies from the top of the wall, and at last he beheld the prairies black with buffalo herds, and the elk gathering upon the edges of the forest. Bears and wolves were closing in from all directions, and now from the sky the Thunder gave his fearful war-whoop, answered by the wolf's long howl.

The badgers and other burrowers began at once to undermine his rocky fortress, while the climbers undertook to scale its perpendicular walls.

Then for the first time on earth the bow was strung, and hundreds of flint-headed arrows found their mark in the bodies of the animals, while each time that the Boy Man swung his stone war-club, his enemies fell in countless numbers.

Finally the insects, the little people of the air, attacked him in a body, filling his eyes and ears, and tormenting him with their poisoned spears, so that he was in despair. He called for help upon his Elder Brother, who ordered him to strike the rocks with his stone war-club. As soon as he had done so, sparks of fire flew upon the dry grass of the prairie and it burst into flame. A mighty smoke ascended, which drove away the teasing swarms of the insect people, while the flames terrified and scattered the others.

This was the first dividing of the trail between man and the animal people, and when the animals had sued for peace, the treaty provided that they must ever after furnish man with flesh for his food and skins for clothing, though not without effort and danger on his part. The little insects refused to make any concession, and have ever since been the tormentors of man; however, the birds of the air declared that they would punish them for their obstinacy, and this they continue to do unto this day. . . .

We had neither devil nor hell in our religion until the white man brought them to us, yet *Unk-to-mee*, the Spider, was doubtless akin to that old Serpent who tempted mother Eve. He is always characterized as tricky, treacherous, and at the same time affable and charming, being not without the gifts of wit, prophecy, and eloquence. He is an adroit magician, able to assume almost any form at will, and impervious to any amount of ridicule and insult. Here we have, it appears, the elements of the story in Genesis; the primal Eden, the tempter in animal form, and the bringing of sorrow and death upon earth through the elemental sins of envy and jealousy.

The warning conveyed in the story of *Unk-to-mee* was ever used with success by Indian parents, and especially grandparents, in the instruction of their children. *Ish-na-e-cha-ge,* on the other hand, was a demigod and mysterious teacher, whose function it was to initiate the first man into his tasks and pleasures here on earth. . . .

On the Border-Land of Spirits

Death and Funeral Customs. The Sacred Lock of Hair. Reincarnation and the Converse of Spirits. Occult and Psychic Powers. The Gift of Prophecy.

The attitude of the Indian toward death, the test and background of life, is entirely consistent with his character and philosophy. Death has no terrors for him; he meets it with simplicity and perfect calm, seeking only an honorable end as his last gift to his family and descendants. Therefore, he courts death in battle; on the other hand, he would regard it as disgraceful to be killed in a private quarrel. If one were dying at home, it is customary to carry his bed out of doors as the end approaches, that his spirit may pass under the open sky.

Next to this, the matter that concerns him most is the parting with his dear ones, especially if he has any little children who must be left behind to suffer want. His family affections are strong, and he grieves intensely for the lost, even though he has unbounded faith in a spiritual companionship.

The outward signs of mourning for the dead are far more spontaneous and convincing than is the correct and well-ordered black of civilization. Both men and women among us loosen their hair and cut it according to the degree of relationship or of devotion. Consistent with the idea of sacrificing all personal beauty and adornment, they trim off likewise from the dress its fringes and ornaments, perhaps cut it short, or cut the robe or blanket in two. The men blacken their faces, and widows or bereaved parents sometimes gash their arms and legs till they are covered with blood. Giving themselves up wholly to their grief, they are no longer concerned about any earthly possession, and often give away all that they have to the first comers, even to their beds and their home. Finally, the wailing for the dead is continued night and day to the point of utter voicelessness; a musical, weird, and heart-piercing sound, which has been compared to the, "keening" of the Celtic mourner.

The old-time burial of the Plains Indians was upon a scaffold of poles, or a platform among the boughs of a tree—their only means of placing the body out of reach of wild beasts, as they had no implements with which to dig a suitable grave. It was prepared by dressing in the finest clothes, together with some personal possessions and ornaments, wrapped in several robes, and finally in a secure covering of raw-hide. As a special mark of respect, the body of a young woman or a warrior was sometimes laid out in state in a new teepee, with the usual household articles and even with a dish of food left beside it, not that they supposed the spirit could use the implements or eat the food, but merely as a last tribute. Then the whole people would break camp and depart to a distance, leaving the dead alone in an honorable solitude.

There was no prescribed ceremony of burial, though the body was carried out with more or less solemnity by selected young men, and sometimes noted warriors were the pall-bearers of a man of distinction. It was usual to choose a prominent hill with a commanding outlook for the last resting-place of our dead. If a man were slain in battle, it was an old custom to place his body against a tree or rock in a sitting position, always facing the enemy, to indicate his undaunted defiance and bravery, even in death.

I recall a touching custom among us, which was designed to keep the memory of the departed near and warm in the bereaved household. A lock of hair of the beloved dead was wrapped in pretty clothing, such as it was supposed that he or she would like to wear if living. This "spirit bundle," as it was called, was suspended from a tripod, and occupied a certain place in the lodge which was the place of honor. At every meal time, a dish of food was placed under it, and some person of the same sex and age as the one who was gone must afterward be invited in to partake of the food. At the end of a year from the time of death, the relatives made a public feast and gave away the clothing and other gifts, while the lock of hair was interred with appropriate ceremonies.

Certainly the Indian never doubted the immortal nature of the spirit or soul of man, but neither did he care to speculate upon its probable state or condition in a future life. The idea of a "happy hunting-ground" is modern and probably borrowed, or invented by the white man. The primitive Indian was content to believe that the spirit which the "Great Mystery" breathed into man returns to Him who gave it, and that after it is freed from the body, it is everywhere and pervades all nature, yet often lingers near the grave or "spirit bundle" for the consolation of friends, and is able to hear prayers. So much of reverence was due the disembodied spirit, that it was not customary with us even to name the dead aloud.

It is well known that the American Indian had somehow developed occult power, and although in the latter days there have been many impostors, and, allowing for the vanity and weakness of human nature, it is fair to assume that there must have been some even in the old days, yet there are well-attest-

ed instances of remarkable prophecies and other mystic practice.

A Sioux prophet predicted the coming of the white man
fully fifty years before the event, and even described accurately his garments and weapons. Before the steamboat was
invented, another prophet of our race described the "Fire
Boat" that would swim upon their mighty river, the
Mississippi, and the date of this prophecy is attested by the
term used, which is long since obsolete. No doubt, many pre-
dictions have been colored to suit the new age, and unques-
tionably false prophets, fakirs, and conjurers have become
the pest of the tribes during the transition period.
Nevertheless, even during this period there was here and
there a man of the old type who was implicitly believed in to
the last.

Notable among these was Ta-chank-pee Ho-tank-a, or His
War Club Speaks Loud, who foretold a year in advance the
details of a great war-party against the Ojibways. There were
to be seven battles, all successful except the last, in which the
Sioux were to be taken at a disadvantage and suffer crushing
defeat. This was carried out to the letter. Our people surprised and slew many of the Ojibways in their villages, but in
turn were followed and cunningly led into an ambush
whence but few came out alive. This was only one of his
remarkable prophecies.

Another famous "medicine-man" was born on the Rum
River about one hundred and fifty years ago, and lived to be
over a century old. He was born during a desperate battle
with the Ojibways, at a moment when, as it seemed, the band
of Sioux engaged were to be annihilated. Therefore the
child's grandmother exclaimed: "Since we are all to perish,
let him die a warrior's death in the field!" and she placed his
cradle under fire, near the spot where his uncle and grandfathers were fighting, for he had no father. But when an old
man discovered the newborn child, he commanded the
women to take care of him, "for," said he, "we know not how

precious the strength of even one warrior may some day become to his nation!"

This child lived to become great among us, as was intimated to the superstitious by the circumstances of his birth. At the age of about seventy-five years, he saved his band from utter destruction at the hands of their ancestral enemies, by suddenly giving warning received in a dream of the approach of a large war-party. The men immediately sent out scouts, and felled trees for a stockade, barely in time to meet and repel the predicted attack. Five years later, he repeated the service, and again saved his people from awful slaughter. There was no confusion of figures or omens, as with lesser medicine-men, but in every incident that is told of him his interpretation of the sign, whatever it was, proved singularly correct.

The father of Little Crow, the chief who led the "Minnesota massacre" of 1862, was another prophet of some note. One of his characteristic prophecies was made only a few years before he died, when he had declared that, although already an old man, he would go once more upon the war-path. At the final war-feast, he declared that three of the enemy would be slain, but he showed great distress and reluctance in foretelling that he would lose two of his own men. Three of the Ojibways were indeed slain as he had said, but in the battle the old war prophet lost both of his two sons.

There are many trustworthy men, and men of Christian faith, to vouch for these and similar events occurring foretold. I cannot pretend to explain them, but I know that our people possessed remarkable powers of concentration and abstraction. I sometimes fancy that such nearness to nature as I have described keeps the spirit sensitive to impressions not commonly felt, and in touch with the unseen powers. Some of us seemed to have a peculiar intuition for the locality of a grave, which they explained by saying they had received a communication from the spirit of the departed. My own grandmother was one of these, and as far back as I can remember, when camping in a strange country, my brother and I would search for and find human bones at the spot she had indicated to us as an ancient burial-place or the spot where a lone warrior had fallen. Of course, the outward signs of burial had been long since obliterated.

The Scotch would certainly have declared that she had the "second sight," for she had other remarkable premonitions or intuitions within my own recollection. I have heard her speak of a peculiar sensation in the breast, by which, as she said, she was advised of anything of importance concerning her absent children. Other native women have claimed a similar monitor, but I never heard of one who could interpret with such accuracy. We were once camping on Lake Manitoba we received news that my uncle and his family had been murdered several weeks before, at a fort some two hundred miles distant. While all our clan were wailing mourning their loss, my grandmother calmly bade them cease, saying that her son was approaching and that they would see him shortly. Although we had no other reason to doubt the ill tidings, it is a fact that my uncle came into camp two days after his reported death.

At another time, when I was fourteen years old, we had just left Fort Ellis on the Assiniboine River, and my youngest uncle had selected a fine spot for our night camp. It was already after sundown, but my grandmother became unaccountably nervous, and positively refused to pitch her tent. So we reluctantly went on down the river, and camped after dark at a secluded place. The next day we learned that a family who were following close behind had stopped at the place first selected by my uncle, but were surprised in the night by a roving war-party, and massacred to a man. This incident made a great impression upon our people.

Many of the Indians believed that one may be born more than once, and there were some who claimed to have full knowledge of a former incarnation. There were also those who held converse with a "twin spirit," who had been born into another tribe or race. There was a well-known Sioux war-prophet who lived in the middle of the last century, so that he is still remembered by the old men of his band. After he had reached middle age, he declared that he had a spirit brother among the Ojibways, the ancestral enemies of the Sioux. He even named the band to which his brother belonged, and said that he also was a war-prophet among his people.

Upon one of their hunts along the border between the two tribes, the Sioux leader one evening called his warriors together, and solemnly declared to them that they were about to meet a like band of Ojibway hunters, led by his spirit twin. Since this was to be their first meeting since they were born as strangers, he earnestly begged the young men to resist the temptation to join battle with their tribal foes.

"You will know him at once," the prophet said to them, "for he will not only look like me in face and form, but he will display the same totem, and even sing my war songs!"

They sent out scouts, who soon returned with news of the approaching party. Then the leading men started with their peace-pipe for the Ojibway camp, and when they were near at hand they fired three distinct volleys, a signal of their desire for a peaceful meeting.

The response came in like manner, and they entered the camp, with the peace-pipe in the hands of the prophet.

Lo, the stranger prophet advanced to meet them, and the people were greatly struck with the resemblance between the two men, who met and embraced one another with unusual fervor.

It was quickly agreed by both parties that they should camp together for several days, and one evening the Sioux made a "warriors' feast" to which they invited many of the Ojibways. The prophet asked his twin brother to sing one of his sacred songs, and behold! it was the very song that he himself was wont to sing. This proved to the warriors beyond doubt or cavil the claims of their seer.

Such are the beliefs in which I was reared—the secret ideals which have nourished in the American Indian a unique character among the peoples of the earth. Its simplicity, its reverence, its bravery and uprightness must be left to make their own appeal to the American of to-day, who is the inheritor of our homes, our names, and our traditions. Since there is nothing left us but remembrance, at least let that remembrance be just!

Selections from

The Indian Today

The Past and Future of the First American

1915

The Indian As He Was

It is the aim of this book to set forth the present status and outlook of the North American Indian. In one sense his is a "vanishing race." In another and an equally true sense it is a thoroughly progressive one, increasing in numbers and vitality, and awakening to the demands of a new life. It is time to ask: What is his national asset? What position does he fill in the body politic? What does he contribute, if anything, to the essential resources of the American nation?

In order to answer these questions, we ought, first, to consider fairly his native environment, temperament, training, and ability in his own lines, before he resigned himself to the inevitable and made up his mind to enter fully into membership in this great and composite nation. If we can see him as he was, we shall be the better able to see him as he is, and by the worth of his native excellence measure his contribution to the common stock.

In the first place, he is free born, hence a free thinker. His government is a pure democracy, based solidly upon intrinsic right and justice, which governs, in his conception, the play of life. I use the word "play" rather than a more pretentious term, as better expressing the trend of his philosophy. He stands naked and upright, both literally and symbolically, before his "Great Mystery." When he fails in obedience, either to natural law (which is supreme law), or to the simple code of his brother man, he will not excuse himself upon a technicality or lie to save his miserable body. He comes to

43

trial and punishment, even to death, if need be, unattended, and as cheerfully as to a council or feast.

As a free man himself, he allows others the same freedom. With him the spiritual life is paramount, and all material things are only means to the end of its ultimate perfection. Daily he meets the "Great Mystery" at morning and evening from the highest hilltop in the region of his home. His attitude toward Deity is simple and childlike.

Social life is kept as simple as possible, freedom of action only curbed by reverence for Those Above, and respect for the purity and perfection of his own body and those of his fellow-creatures. Only such laws are made as have been found necessary to guard personal and tribal purity and honor. The women do not associate freely with men outside of the family, and even within it strict decorum is observed between grown brothers and sisters. Birth and marriage are guarded with a peculiar sacredness as mysterious events. Strenuous out-of-door life and the discipline of war subdue the physical appetites of the men, and self-control is regarded as a religious duty. Among the Sioux it was originally held that children should not be born into a family oftener than once in three years, and no woman was expected to bear more than five children, for whom both masculine and feminine names were provided to indicate the order of their birth.

The Indian, in his simple philosophy, was careful to avoid a centralized population, wherein lies civilization's devil. He would not be forced to accept materialism as the basic principle of his life, but preferred to reduce existence to its simplest terms. His roving out-of-door life was more precarious, no doubt, than life reduced to a system, a mechanical routine; yet in his view it was and is infinitely happier. To be sure, this philosophy of his had its disadvantages and obvious defects, yet it was reasonably consistent with itself, which is more than can be said for our modern civilization. He knew that virtue is essential to the maintenance of physical excellence, and that strength, in the sense of endurance and vitality, underlies all genuine beauty. He was as a rule prepared to volunteer his services at any time in behalf of his fellows, at any cost of inconvenience and real hardship, and thus to grow in personality and soul-culture. Generous to the last mouthful of food, fearless of hunger, suffering, and death, he was surely something of a hero. Not "to have," but "to be," was his national motto.

As parents are responsible for the conduct of their children, so was the Indian clan responsible for the behavior of its members, both among themselves and in relation to other clans. This simple family government extended throughout the bands, tribes, and nations. There was no "politics" and no money in it for any one. The conscience was never at war with the mind, and no undue advantage was sought by any individual. Justice must be impartial; hence if the accused alone knew the facts, it was a common thing for him to surrender himself.

Intertribal Warfare

As regards the original Indian warfare, it was founded upon the principle of manly rivalry in patriotism, bravery, and self-sacrifice. The willingness to risk life for the welfare or honor of the people was the highest test of character. In order that the reputations thus gained might be preserved as an example to the young, a system of decorations was evolved, including the symbolic wearing of certain feathers and skins, especially eagle feathers, and the conferring of "honor names" for special exploits. These distinctions could not be gained unjustly or by favoritism, as is often the case with rank and honors among civilized men, since the deeds claimed must be proved by witnesses before the grand council of war chiefs. If one strikes an enemy in battle, whether he kills him or not, he must announce the fact in a loud voice, so that it may be noted and remembered. The danger and difficulty is regarded above the amount of damage inflicted upon the enemy, and a man may wear the eagle plumes who has never taken a life.

It is easily seen that these intertribal contests were not based upon the same motives nor waged for the same objects as the wars of civilization—namely, for spoil and territorial aggrandizement. There was no mass play; army was not pitted against army; individual valor was held in highest regard. It was not usual to take captives, except occasionally of women and children, who were adopted into the tribe and treated with kindness. There was no traffic in the labor or flesh of prisoners. Such warfare, in fact, was scarcely more than a series of duels or irregular skirmishes, engaged in by individuals and small groups, and in many cases was but little rougher than a game of university football. Some were killed because they were caught, or proved weaker and less athletic than their opponents. It was one way of disciplining a man and working off the superfluous energy that might otherwise lead to domestic quarrels. If he met his equal or superior and was slain, fighting bravely to the end, his friends might weep honorable tears.

The only atrocity of this early warfare was the taking of a small scalp lock by the leader, as a semi-religious trophy of the event; and as long as it was preserved, the Sioux warriors wore mourning for their dead enemy. Not all the tribes took scalps. It was only after the bounties offered by the colonial governments, notably in Massachusetts and Pennsylvania, for scalps of women and children as well as men, that the practice became general, and led to further mutilations, often stigmatized as "Indian," though in reality they have been practiced by so-called civilized nations down to a recent period. That one should do murder for pay is not an Indian idea but one imposed upon the race by white barbarians.

It was a custom of the Plains Indians to hold peaceful meetings in summer, at which times they would vie with one another in friendliness and generosity. Each family would single out a family of another tribe as special guests of honor.

Valuable horses and richly adorned garments were freely given at the feasts and dances. During these intertribal reunions the contests between the tribes were recalled and their events rehearsed, the dead heroes on both sides receiving special tributes of honor. Parents would entertain the participants in an engagement in which their son had fallen, perhaps, the year before, giving lavish hospitality and handsome presents in token that all was done in fair fight, and there remained no ill feeling.

First Effects of Civilization

Whatever may be said for this scheme of life, its weaknesses are very apparent, and resulted in its early fall when confronted with the complicated system of so-called civilization. With us the individual was supreme; all combination was voluntary in its nature; there was no commerce worthy of the name, no national wealth, no taxation for the support of government, and the chiefs were merely natural leaders with much influence but little authority. The system worked well with men who were all of the same mind, but in the face of a powerful government and an organized army it quickly disintegrated and collapsed. Could the many small tribes and bands have formed a stable combination or league, they might have successfully resisted the invader; but instead they stood separately, though too weak to maintain their dignity by force, and in many cases entered upon a devastating warfare with one another, using the new and more deadly weapons, thus destroying one another. Since there was no central government, but a series of loose confederations of linguistic or allied groups, each of which had its titular head, able to make treaties or to declare war, these bands were met and subdued one at a time.

The original North American knew no fermented or spirituous drink. To be sure, he used a mild narcotic—tobacco mixed with aromatic leaves or bark, and smoked in strict moderation, generally as a semi-religious ceremony. Though wild grapes were found here in abundance, none had ever made wine from them. The introduction of liquor completed the ruin of our race.

During a long period the fur trade was an important factor in the world's commerce, and accordingly the friendship and favor of the natives were eagerly sought by the leading nations of Europe. Great use was made of whiskey and gunpowder as articles of trade. Demoralization was rapid. Many tribes were decimated and others wiped out entirely by the ravages of strong drink and disease, especially smallpox and cholera. The former was terribly fatal. The Indians knew nothing of its nature or treatment, and during the nineteenth century the tribes along the Mississippi and Missouri rivers suffered severely. Even in my own day I have seen and talked with the few desolate survivors of a thriving village.

In the decade following 1840, cholera ravaged the tribes dwelling along the great waterways. Venereal disease followed upon the frequent immoralities of white soldiers and frontiersmen. As soon as the Indian came into the reservation and adopted an indoor mode of life, bronchitis and pneumonia worked havoc with him, and that scourge of the present-day red man, tuberculosis, took its rise then in overcrowded log cabins and unsanitary living, together with insufficient and often unwholesome food. During this period there was a rapid decline in the Indian population, leading to the now discredited theory that the race was necessarily "dying out" from contact with civilization.

It must always be borne in mind that the *first* effect of association with the more advanced race was not improvement but degeneracy. I have no wish to discredit the statements of the early explorers, including the Jesuit priests; but it is evident that in the zeal of the latter to gain honor for their society for saving the souls of the natives it was almost necessary to represent them as godless and murderous savages—otherwise there would be no one to convert!

Of course they were not angels, but I think I have made it clear that they were a God-fearing, clean, and honorable people before the coming of the white man.

The Transition Period

The transition from their natural life to the artificial life of civilization has been very gradual in most cases, until the last fifty years, when the changes have been more rapid. Those who were first affected were the so-called "Five Civilized Nations" of the South, and the "Six Nations" of New York State, together with some of the now extinct bands in New England, who came in close touch with the early colonists. Both politically and commercially, they played an important part in the settlement of America. Their services as scouts, guides, and allies were of great value in the early history of this country, and down to recent years. Many received no salary, and some even furnished their own horses. It is a remarkable fact that there is not one instance on record of a scout betraying the cause he served, even though used against his own tribe and his own relatives. Once his honor is pledged to a public trust, he must sustain it at any cost.

In many cases those tribes which declared allegiance to the French, the English, or the Americans, were in their turn the means of bringing a neighboring tribe into subjection. Thus began a new era in the history of the Indian, inaugurating a kind of warfare that was cruel, relentless, and demoralizing, since it was based upon the desire to conquer and to despoil the conquered of his possessions—a motive unknown to the primitive American.

To be sure the new weapons were more efficient, and therefore more deadly; the new clothing was gayer, but less perfectly adapted to the purposes of primitive life. Indeed, the buckskin clothing and moccasins of the Indian were very generally adopted by the white frontiersman. On the other hand, his spiritual and moral loss was great. He who listened to the preaching of the missionaries came to believe that the white man alone has a real God, and that the things he had hitherto held sacred are inventions of the devil. This undermined the foundations of his philosophy, and very often without substituting for it the Christian philosophy, which the inconsistency of its advocates, rather than any innate quality, made it difficult for him to accept or understand.

A few did, in good faith, accept the white man's God. The black-robed preacher was like the Indian himself in seeking no soft things, and as he followed the fortunes of the tribes in the wilderness, the tribesmen learned to trust and to love him. Then came other missionaries who had houses to sleep in, and gardens planted, and who hesitated to sleep in the Indian's wigwam or eat of his wild meat, but for the most part held themselves aloof and urged their own dress and ways upon their converts. These, too, had their following in due time. But in the main it is true that while the Indian eagerly sought guns and gunpowder, knives and whiskey, a few articles of dress, and, later, horses, he did not of himself desire the white man's food, his houses, his books, his government, or his religion.

The two great "civilizers," after all, were whiskey and gunpowder, and from the hour the red man accepted these he had in reality sold his birthright, and all unconsciously consented to his own ruin. Immediately his manhood began to crumble. . . .

Intermarriages were not common among the different tribes in the old days, and still less so between Indians and Caucasians. The earlier intermarriages were with the higher class of Europeans: officers, noblemen, etc., and many of the offspring of these unions were highly esteemed, some becoming chiefs. At this period the natives preferred their own marriage customs, which was convenient for the white officers who were thus enabled to desert their wives and children when they chose, and often did so, quite as if there were no binding obligation. Later, when unions between the lower class of both races became common, the Sioux refused to recognize their half-breeds as members of the tribe, and a certain territory was set apart for them. . . .

This transition period has been a time of stress and suffering for my people. Once they had departed from the broad democracy and pure idealism of their prime, and undertaken to enter upon the world-game of competition, their rudder was unshipped, their compass lost, and the whirlwind and tempest of materialism and love of conquest tossed them to and fro like leaves in the wind.

"You are a child," said the white man in effect to the simple and credulous native. "You cannot make or invent anything. We have the only God, and he has given us authority to teach and to govern all the peoples of the earth. In proof of this we have His Book, a supernatural guide, every word of which is true and binding. We are a superior race—a chosen people. We have a heaven fenced in with golden gates from all pagans and unbelievers, and a hell where the souls of such are tortured eternally. We are honorable, truthful, refined, religious, peaceful; we hate cruelty and injustice; our business is to educate, Christianize, and protect the rights and property of the weak and the uncivilized."

This sort of talk had its effect. Let us see what followed.

The How and the Why of Indian Wars

I have tried to set forth the character and motives of the primitive Indian as they were affected by contact with civilization. In a word, demoralization was gradual but certain, culminating in the final loss of his freedom and confinement to the reservation under most depressing conditions. It must be borne in mind that there has been scarcely any genuine wild life among us for the past thirty-five years.* Sitting Bull's band of Sioux were the last real hostiles of their tribe to surrender, in 1880, and Geronimo's Apaches followed in 1886. . . .

* editor's note: from 1880 to 1915.

It is important to understand the underlying causes of Indian wars. There are people today who believe that the Indian likes nothing better than going on the warpath, killing and scalping from sheer native cruelty and lust for blood. His character as a man of peace has not been appreciated. Yet it is a matter of history that the newcomers were welcomed in almost every case with unsuspecting kindness, and in his dealings with the white man the original owner of the soil has been uniformly patient and reasonable, offering resistance only under irresistible provocation . . .

The New Indian Policy

The Wars of the Sects

Nevertheless it was largely through the influence of the missionaries and their converts that in most of the treaties made during this period there were inserted clauses providing for the practical education of the Indian children. There has been much fraud connected with the purchase of materials and supplies, and in every way that shrewd and unprincipled men can devise, but even the politicians could not entirely prevent the building of those schools. One fact stands out boldly: it was the Christian missionary, in spite of serious mistakes, who played the most important part in the transformation of the Indian and the development of the West.

Modern "Friends of the Indian"

. . . To sum up, he (the Indian race) had been an indomitable foe, and occupied a vast region which by 1870 was already beat upon by the tides of settlement. Two things were determined upon: First, he must be induced, bribed, or forced to enter the reservation. Second, he must be trained and persuaded to adopt civilized life, and so saved to the future if he proved to be worth saving, which many doubted.

In order to carry out these projects his wild food supply had to be ruthlessly cut off, and the buffalo were of necessity sacrificed.

Here is a system which has gradually taken its present complicated form during two thousand years. A primitive race has put it on ready made, to a large extent, within two generations. In order to accomplish such a feat, they had to fight physical demoralization, psychological confusion, and spiritual apathy. In other words, the old building had to be pulled down, foundations and all, and replaced by the new. But you have had to use the same timber! . . .

The Indian at Home

Although among the graduates and ex-students of the Indian schools there are now some in almost every modern occupation, including commerce, the trades and professions, the great majority of these young people, as of their fellow tribesmen who lack an English education, are farmers, ranchers, and stockmen. Nearly all Indians own some land, either individually or in common; and while it may generally be leased by those who are either unable or for good reasons do not desire to work it themselves, this is done under such troublesome restrictions and conditions that it is, as a general rule, better for the owner to live on and utilize his allotment. Of course this is a rule that admits of many exceptions. . . .

The Problem of Self-Support

Since most Indian reservations are in the arid belt and the greater portion of the land is therefore unsuited to agriculture, at least without extensive irrigation, perhaps the larger number of the men are stock-raisers, an occupation well suited to the Plains Indians, who are great riders and very fond of their horses. They raise both horses and cattle . . .

Indian Woman as Home-Makers

Probably the average white man still believes that the Indian woman of the old days was little more than a beast of burden to her husband. But the missionary who has lived among his people, the sympathetic observer of their everyday life, holds a very different opinion. You may generally see the mother and her babe folded close in one shawl, indicating the real and most important business of her existence. Without the child, life is but a hollow play, and all Indians pity the couple who are unable to obey the primary command, the first law of real happiness.

She has always been the silent but telling power behind life's activities, and at the same time shared equally with her mate the arduous duties of primitive society. Possessed of true feminine dignity and modesty, she was expected to be his equal in physical endurance and skill, but his superior in spiritual insight. She was looked to for the endowment of her child with nature's gifts and powers, and no woman of any race has ever come closer to universal motherhood.

She was the spiritual teacher of the child, as well as its tender nurse, and she brought its developing soul before the "Great Mystery" as soon as she was aware of its coming. When she had finished her work, at the age of five to eight years, she turned her boy over to his father for manly training, and to the grandparents for traditional instruction, but the girl child remained under her close and thoughtful supervision. She preserved man from soul-killing materialism by herself owning what few possessions they had, and thus branding possession as feminine. The movable home was hers, with all its belongings, and she ruled there unquestioned. She was, in fact, the moral salvation of the race; all virtue was entrusted to her, and her position was recognized by all. It was held in all gentleness and discretion, under the rule that no woman could talk much or loudly until she became a grandmother.

The Indian woman suffered greatly during the transition period of civilization, when men were demoralized by whiskey, and possession became masculine. The division of labor did not readily adjust itself to the change, so that her burdens were multiplied while her influence decreased. Tribe after tribe underwent the catastrophe of a disorganized and disunited family life. . . .

As the men have gradually assumed the responsibility of the outdoor toil, cultivating the fields and building the houses, the women have undertaken the complicated housekeeping tasks of their white sisters. It is true that until they understood the civilized way of cooking and the sanitation of stationary homes, the race declined in health and vigor. . . .

The Indian as a Citizen

We have taken note of the reluctance of the American Indian to develop an organized community life, though few appreciate his reasons for preferring a simpler social ideal. As a matter of fact as well as sentiment, he was well content with his own customs and philosophy. Nevertheless, after due protest and resistance, he has accepted the situation; and, having accepted it, he is found to be easily governed by civilized law and usages. It has been demonstrated more than once that he is capable of sustaining a high moral and social standard when placed under wise guidance and at the same time protected from the barbarians of civilization. . . .

Native Arts and Industries

In his sense of the aesthetic, which is closely akin to religious feeling, the American Indian stands alone. In accord with his nature and beliefs, he does not pretend to imitate the inimitable, or to reproduce exactly the work of the Great Artist. That which is beautiful must not be trafficked with, but must only be reverenced and adored. It must appear in speech and action. The symmetrical and graceful body must express something of it. Beauty, in our eyes, is always fresh and living, even as God Himself dresses the world anew at each season of the year.

It may be artistic to imitate nature and even try to improve upon her, but we Indians think it very tiresome, especially as one considers the material side of the work—the pigment, the brush, the canvas! There is no mystery there; you know all about them! Worst of all is the commercialization of art. The rudely carved totem pole may appear grotesque to the white man, but it is the sincere expression of the faith and personality of the Indian craftsman, and has never been sold or bartered until it reached civilization.

The Indian's Viewpoint

Now we see at once the root of the red man's failure to approach even distantly the artistic standard of the civilized world. It lies not in the lack of creative imagination—for in this quality he is a born artist—it lies rather in his point of view. I once showed a party of Sioux chiefs the sights of Washington, and endeavored to impress them with the wonderful achievements of civilization. After visiting the Capitol and other famous buildings, we passed through the Corcoran Art Gallery, where I tried to explain how the white man valued this or that painting as a work of genius and a masterpiece of art.

"Ah!" exclaimed an old man, "such is the strange philosophy of the white man! He hews down the forest that has stood for centuries in its pride and grandeur, tears up the bosom of mother earth, and causes the silvery watercourses to waste and vanish away. He ruthlessly disfigures God's own pictures and monuments, and then daubs a flat surface with many colors, and praises his work as a masterpiece!"

This is the spirit of the original American. He holds nature to be the measure of consummate beauty, and its destruction as sacrilege. I have seen in our midsummer celebrations cool arbors built of fresh-cut branches for council and dance halls, while those who attended decked themselves with leafy boughs, carrying shields and fans of the same, and even making wreaths for their horses' necks. But, strange to say, they seldom made a free use of flowers. I once asked the reason of this.

"Why," said one, "the flowers are for our souls to enjoy; not for our bodies to wear. Leave them alone and they will live out their lives and reproduce themselves as the Great Gardener intended. He planted them: we must not pluck them, for it would be selfish to do so."

Indian beadwork in leaf and flower designs is generally modern. The old-time patterns are for the most part simple geometrical figures, which are decorative and emblematic rather than imitative. Shafts of light and shadow alternating or dovetailed represent life, its joys and sorrows. The world is conceived of as rectangular and flat, and is represented by a square. The sky is concave—a hollow sphere. A drawing of the horizon line colored pale yellow stands for dawn; colored red, for sunset. Day is blue, and night black spangled with stars. Lightning, rain, wind, water, mountains, and many other natural features or elements are symbolized rather than copied literally upon many sorts of Indian handiwork. Animal figures are drawn in such a manner as to give expression to the type or spirit of the animal rather than its body, emphasizing the head with the horns, or any distinguishing feature. These designs have a religious significance and furnish the individual with his personal and clan emblem, or coat of arms.

Symbolic decorations are used on blankets, baskets, pottery, and garments of ceremony to be worn at rituals and public functions. Sometimes a man's teepee is decorated in accordance with the standing of the owner. Weapons of war are adorned with emblems, and also pipes, or calumets, but not the every-day weapons used in hunting. The war steed is decorated equally with his rider, and sometimes wears the feathers that signify degrees of honor.

The Woman and her Craftsmanship

In his weaving, painting, and embroidery of beads and quills the red man has shown a marked color sense, and his blending of brilliant hues is subtle and Oriental in effect. The women did most of this work and displayed vast ingenuity in the selection of native materials and dyes. A variety of beautiful grasses, roots, and barks are used for baskets by the different tribes, and some even used gorgeous feathers for extra ornamentation. Each was perfectly adapted in style, size, and form to its intended use.

Pottery was made by the women of the southwest for household furniture and utensils, and their vessels, burned in crude furnaces, were often gracefully shaped and exquisitely decorated. The designs were both imprinted on the soft clay and modeled in relief. The nomadic tribes of the plains could not well carry these fragile wares with them on their wanderings, and accordingly their dishes were mainly of bark and wood, the latter sometimes carved. Spoons were prettily made of translucent horn. They were fond of painting their rawhide cases in brilliant colors. The most famous blankets are made by the Navajoes upon rude hand looms and are wonderfully fine in weave, color, and design.

This native skill combined with love of the work and perfect sincerity—the qualities which still make the Indian woman's blanket or basket or bowl or moccasins of the old type so highly prized—are among the precious things lost or sacrificed to the advance of an alien civilization. Cheap machine-made garments and utensils, without beauty or durability, have crowded out the old; and where the women still ply their ancient trade, they do it now for money, not for love, and in most cases use modern materials and patterns, even imported yarns and "Diamond dyes!" Genuine curios or antiques are already becoming very rare, except in museums, and sometimes command fabulous prices. As the older generation passes, there is danger of losing altogether the secret of Indian art and craftsmanship.

Modern Indian Art

Struck by this danger, and realizing the innate charm of the work and its adaptability to modem demands, a few enthusiasts have made of late years an effort to preserve and extend it, both in order that a distinctive and vitally American art-form may not disappear, and as a means of self-support for Indian women. Depots or stores have been established at various points for the purpose of encouraging such manufactures and of finding a market for them, not so much from commercial as from artistic and philanthropic motives. . . .

The Indian did not paint nature, not because he did not feel it, but because it was sacred to him. He so loved the reality that he could not venture upon the imitation. It is now time to unfold the resources of his genius, locked up for untold ages by the usages and philosophy of his people. They held it sacrilege to reproduce the exact likeness of the human form or face. This is the reason that early attempts to paint the natives were attended with difficulty, and there are still Indians who refuse to be photographed.

Music, Dancing, Dramatic Art

A form of self-expression which has always been characteristic of my race is found in their music. In music is the very soul of the Indian; yet the civilized nations have but recently discovered that such a thing exists! His chants are simple, expressive, and haunting in quality, and voice his inmost feelings, grave or gay, in every emotion and situation in life. They vary much with tribes and even with individuals. A man often composes his own song, which belongs to him and is deeply imbued with his personality. These songs are frequently without words, the meaning being too profound for words; they are direct emanations of the human spirit. If words are used, they are few and symbolic in character. There is no definite harmony in the songs—only rhythm and melody, and there are striking variations of time and intonation which render them difficult to the "civilized" ear.

Nevertheless, within the last few years there has been a serious effort to collect these wild folksongs of the woods and plains by means of notation and the phonograph, and in some cases this has been connected with the attempt to harmonize and popularize them. . . .

Useful Arts and Inventions

Among native inventions which have been of conspicuous use and value to the dispossessors of the Indian we recollect at once the bark canoe, the snowshoe, the moccasin (called the most perfect footwear ever invented), the game of lacrosse and probably other games, also the conical teepee which served as a model for the Sibley army tent. Pemmican, a condensed food made of pounded dried meat combined with melted fat and dried fruits, has been largely utilized by recent polar explorers.

The art of sugar making from the sap of the hard or sugar maple was first taught by the aborigines to the white settlers. In my day the Sioux used also the box elder for sugar making, and from the birch and ash is made a dark-colored sugar that was used by them as a carrier in medicine. However, none of these yield as freely as the maple. The Ojibways of Minnesota still make and sell delicious maple sugar, put up in "*mococks*," or birch-bark packages. Their wild rice, a native grain of remarkably fine flavor and nutritious qualities, is also in a small way an article of commerce. It really ought to be grown on a large scale and popularized as a package cereal. A large fortune doubtless awaits the lucky exploiter of this distinctive "breakfast food."

In agriculture the achievements of the Indian have probably been underestimated, although it is well known that the Indian corn was the mother of all the choice varieties which today form an important source of food supply for the civilized world. The women cultivated the maize with primitive implements, and prepared it for food in many attractive forms, including hominy and succotash, of which the names, as well as the dishes themselves, are borrowed from the red man. . . . Besides maize and tobacco, some tribes, especially in the South, grew native cotton and a variety of fruits and vegetables.

The buckskin clothing of my race was exceedingly practical as well as handsome, and has been adapted to the use of hunters, explorers, and frontiersmen, down to the present day. His feathers and other decorations are imitated by women of fashion, and his moccasin was never so much in vogue as now. The old wooden Indian in front of the tobacco store looks less lonely as he gazes upon a procession of bright-eyed young people, with now and then one older, Indian-clad, joyous, and full of health, returning, if only for a few short weeks, to the life he knew of old.

The Indian's Gifts to the Nation

What does the original American contribute, in the final summing up, to the country of his birth and his adoption? Not much, perhaps, in comparison with the brilliant achievements of civilization; yet, after all, is there not something worthy of perpetuation in the spirit of his democracy—the very essence of patriotism and justice between man and man? Silently, by example only, in wordless patience, he holds stoutly to his native vision. We must admit that the tacit influence of his philosophy has been felt at last, and a self-seeking world has paused in its mad rush to pay him a tribute.

Yes, the world has recognized his type, seized his point of view. We have lived to see monuments erected to his memory. The painter, sculptor, author, scientist, preacher, all have found in him a model worthy of study and serious presentation. . . .

No longer does the red man live alone in the blood-curdling pages of the sensational story-writer. He is the subject of profound study as a man, a philosopher, a noble type both physically and spiritually. Symmetrical and finely poised in body, the same is true of his character. He stands naked before you, scorning the garb of deception and pretense, for he is a true child of nature.

How has he contributed to the world's progress? By his personal faithfulness to duty and devotion to a trust. He has not advertised his faithfulness nor made capital of his honor. Again and again he has proved his worth as a citizen of his country and of the world by his constancy in the face of hardship and death. Racial antagonism was to him no excuse for breaking his word. This simplicity and fairness has cost him dear; it cost his country and his freedom, even the extinction of his race as a separate and peculiar people; but as a type, an ideal, he lives and will live!

The red man's genius for military tactics and strategy has been admitted again and again by those who have fought against him, often unwillingly, because they saw that he was in the right. His long, unequal struggle against the dominant race has produced a brilliant array of notable men without education in letters. Such were King Philip of the Wampanoags; Pontiac, the great Ottawa; Cornplanter of the Senecas, in the eighteenth century; while in the first half of the nineteenth we have Weatherford of the Creeks, Tecumseh of the Shawnees, Little Turtle of the Miamis, Wabashaw and Wanatan of the Sioux, Black Hawk of the Foxes, Osceola of the Seminoles. During the last half of the century there arose another set of Indian leaders, the last of their type—such men as Ouray of the Utes, Geronimo of the Apaches, Red Cloud, Spotted Tail, and Sitting Bull of the Sioux, Chief Joseph of the Nez Perces, and Dull Knife of the Northern Cheyennes. Men like these are an ornament to any country.

It has been said that their generalship was equal to that of Caesar or Napoleon; even greater considering that here was no organization, no treasury, or hope of spoils, or even a stable government behind them. They displayed their leadership under conditions in which Napoleon would have failed. As regards personal bravery, no man could outdo them. After Jackson had defeated the Creeks, he demanded of them the war chief Weatherford, dead or alive. The following night Weatherford presented himself alone at the general's tent, saying: "I am Weatherford; do as you please with me. I would be still fighting you had I the warriors to fight with; but they no longer answer my call, for they are dead."

Chief Joseph, who conducted that masterly retreat of eleven hundred miles, burdened with his women and children, the old men and the wounded, surrendered at last, as he told me in Washington, because he could "bear no longer the sufferings of the innocent." These men were not bloodthirsty or wanton murderers; they were as gentle at home as they were terrific in battle. Chief Joseph would never harm a white woman or child, and more than once helped non-combatants to a place of safety.

In oratory and unstudied eloquence the American Indian has at times equaled even the lofty flights of the Greeks and Romans. The noted Red Jacket, perhaps the greatest orator and philosopher of primitive America, was declared by the late Governor Clinton of New York to be the equal of Demosthenes. President Jefferson called the best-known speech of Logan, the Mingo chief, the "height of human utterance."

Now let us consider some of his definite contributions to the birth and nurture of the United States. We have borrowed his emblem, the American eagle, which matches well his bold and aspiring spirit. It is impossible to forget that his country and its freely offered hospitality are the very foundation of our national existence, but his services as a scout and soldier have scarcely been valued at their true worth.

The Indian Soldier and Scout

. . . The Indian system of scouting has long been recognized as one of the most useful adjuncts of war. His peculiar and efficient methods of communication in the field by means of blanket signals, smoke signals, the arrangement of rockpiles, and by heliograph (small mirrors or reflectors), the last, of course, in more modern days, have all been made use of at one time or another by the United States Army. . . .

I do not wish to disparage any one, but I do say that the virtues claimed by "Christian civilization" are not peculiar to any culture or religion. My people were very simple and unpractical—the modern obstacle to the fulfillment of the Christ ideal. Their strength lay in self-denial. Not only men, but women of the race have served the nation at most opportune moments in the history of this country.

Historic Indian Women

. . . Best of all, perhaps, we are beginning to recognize the Indian's good sense and sanity in the way of simple living and the mastery of the great out of doors. Like him, the wisest Americans are living, playing, and sleeping in the open for at least a part of the year, receiving the vital benefits of the pure air and sunlight. His deeds are carved upon the very rocks; the names he loved to speak are fastened upon the landscape; and he still lives in spirit, silently leading the multitude, for the new generation have taken him for their hero and model.

The Children's Hero

I call upon the parents of America to give their fullest support to those great organizations, the Boy Scouts and the Camp Fire Girls. The young people of today are learning through this movement much of the wisdom of the first American. In the mad rush for wealth we have too long overlooked the foundations of our national welfare. The contribution of the American Indian, though considerable from

any point of view, is not to be measured by material acquirement. Its greatest worth is spiritual and philosophical. He will
live, not only in the splendor of his past, the poetry of his legends and his art, not only in the interfusion of his blood with
yours, and his faithful adherence to the new ideals of
American citizenship, but in the living thought of the nation.

Selections from
Indian Boyhood
1902

Earliest Recollections

Hakadah, 'The Pitiful Last'

What boy would not be an Indian for a while when he thinks of the freest life in the world? This life was mine. Every day there was a real hunt. There was real game. Occasionally there was a medicine dance away off in the woods where no one could disturb us, in which the boys impersonated their elders, Brave Bull, Standing Elk, High Hawk, Medicine Bear, and the rest. They painted and imitated their fathers and grandfathers to the minutest detail, and accurately too, because they had seen the real thing all their lives.

We were not only good mimics, but we were close students of nature. We studied the habits of animals just as you study your books. We watched the men of our people and represented them in our play; then learned to emulate them in our lives.

No people have a better use of their five senses than the children of the wilderness. We could smell as well as hear and see. We could feel and taste as well as we could see and hear. Nowhere has the memory been more fully developed than in the wild life, and I can still see wherein I owe much to my early training.

Of course I myself do not remember when I first saw the day, but my brothers have often recalled the event with much mirth; for it was a custom of the Sioux that when a boy was born his brother must plunge into the water, or roll in the snow naked if it was winter time; and if he was not big enough to do either of these himself, water was thrown on him. If the new-born had a sister, she must be immersed. The idea was that a warrior had come to camp, and the other children must display some act of hardihood.

I was so unfortunate as to be the youngest of five children who, soon after I was born, were left motherless. I had to bear the humiliating name "Hakadah," meaning "the pitiful last," until I should earn a more dignified and appropriate name. I was regarded as little more than a play-thing by the rest of the children.

My mother, who was known as the handsomest woman of all the Spirit Lake and Leaf Dweller Sioux, was dangerously ill, and one of the medicine men who attended her said: "Another medicine man has come into existence, but the mother must die. Therefore let him bear the name 'Mysterious Medicine.'" But one of the bystanders hastily interfered, saying that an uncle of the child already bore that name, so, for the time, I was only "Hakadah."

My beautiful mother, sometimes called the "Demi-Goddess" of the Sioux, who tradition says had every feature of a Caucasian descent with the exception of her luxuriant black hair and deep black eyes, held me tightly to her bosom upon her death-bed, while she whispered a few words to her mother-in-law. She said: "I give you this boy for your own.". . .

The woman to whom these words were spoken was below the average in stature, remarkably active for her age (she was then fully sixty), and possessed of as much goodness as intelligence. . . .

The babe was done up as usual in a movable cradle made from an oak board two and a half feet long and one and a half feet wide. On one side of it was nailed with brass-headed tacks the richly-embroidered sack, which was open in front and laced up and down with buckskin strings. Over the arms of the infant was a wooden bow, the ends of which were firmly attached to the board, so that if the cradle should fall the child's head and face would be protected. On this bow were hung curious playthings—strings of artistically carved bones and hoofs of deer, which rattled when the little hands moved them.

In this upright cradle I lived, played and slept the greater part of the time during the first few months of my life. Whether I was made to lean against a lodge pole or was suspended from a bough of a tree, while my grandmother cut wood, or whether I was carried on her back, or conveniently balanced by another child in a similar cradle hung on the opposite side of a pony, I was still in my oaken bed.

This grandmother, who had already lived through sixty years of hardships, was a wonder to the young maidens of the tribe. She showed no less enthusiasm over Hakadah than she had done when she held her first-born, the boy's father, in her arms. Every little attention that is due to a loved child she performed with much skill and devotion. She made all my scanty garments and my tiny moccasins with a great deal of taste. It was said by all that I could not have had more attention had my mother been living.

Uncheedah (grandmother) was a great singer. Sometimes, when Hakadah wakened too early in the morning, she would sing to him something like the following lullaby:

> Sleep, sleep, my boy, the Chippewas
> Are far away—are far away.
> Sleep, sleep, my boy; prepare to meet
> The foe by day—the foe by day!
> The cowards will not dare to fight
> Till morning break—till morning break.
> Sleep, sleep, my child, while still 'tis night;
> Then bravely wake—then bravely wake!

The Dakota women were wont to cut and bring their fuel from the woods and, in fact, to perform most of the drudgery of the camp. This of necessity fell to their lot, because the men must follow the game during the day. Very often my grandmother carried me with her on these excursions; and while she worked it was her habit to suspend me from a wild grape vine or a springy bough, so that the least breeze would swing the cradle to and fro.

She has told me that when I had grown old enough to take notice, I was apparently capable of holding extended conversations in an unknown dialect with birds and red squir- rels. Once I fell asleep in my cradle, suspended five or six feet from the ground, while Uncheedah was some distance away, gathering birch bark for a canoe. A squirrel had found it con- venient to come upon the bow of my cradle and nibble his hickory nut, until he awoke me by dropping the crumbs of his meal. My disapproval of his intrusion was so decided that he had to take a sudden and quick flight to another bough, and from there he began to pour out his wrath upon me, while I continued my objections to his presence so audibly that Uncheedah soon came to my rescue, and compelled the bold intruder to go away. It was a common thing for birds to alight on my cradle in the woods. . . .

After I left my cradle, I almost walked away from it, she told me. She then began calling my attention to natural objects. Whenever I heard the song of a bird, she would tell me what bird it came from, something after this fashion:

"Hakadah, listen to *Shechoka* (the robin) calling his mate. He says he has just found something good to eat." Or "Listen to *Oopehanska* (the thrush); he is singing for his little wife. He will sing his best." When in the evening the whippoorwill started his song with vim, no further than a stone's throw from our tent in the woods, she would say to me:

"Hush! It may be an Ojibway scout!"

Again, when I waked at midnight, she would say:

"Do not cry! *Hinakaga* (the owl) is watching you from the tree-top."

I usually covered up my head, for I had perfect faith in my grandmother's admonitions, and she had given me a dread- ful idea of this bird. It was one of her legends that a little boy was once standing just outside of the teepee (tent), crying vigorously for his mother, when *Hinakaga* swooped down in the darkness and carried the poor little fellow up into the trees. It was well known that the hoot of the owl was commonly imitated by Indian scouts when on the war-path. There had been dreadful massacres immediately following this call. Therefore it was deemed wise to impress the sound early upon the mind of the child.

Indian children were trained so that they hardly ever cried much in the night. This was very expedient and necessary in their exposed life. In my infancy it was my grandmother's custom to put me to sleep, as she said, with the birds, and to waken me with them, until it became a habit. She did this with an object in view. An Indian must always rise early. In the first place, as a hunter, he finds his game best at daybreak. Secondly, other tribes, when on the war-path, usually make their attack very early in the morning. Even when our people are moving about leisurely, we like to rise before daybreak, in order to travel when the air is cool, and unobserved, perchance, by our enemies.

As a little child, it was instilled into me to be silent and reticent. This was one of the most important traits to form in the character of the Indian. As a hunter and warrior it was considered absolutely necessary to him, and was thought to lay the foundations of patience and self-control. There are times when boisterous mirth is indulged in by our people, but the rule is gravity and decorum.

After all, my babyhood was full of interest and the beginnings of life's realities. The spirit of daring was already whispered into my ears. The value of the eagle feather as worn by the warrior had caught my eye. One day, when I was left alone, at scarcely two years of age, I took my uncle's war bonnet and plucked out all its eagle feathers to decorate my dog and myself. So soon the life that was about me had made its impress, and already I desired intensely to comply with all of its demands.

Early Hardships

One of the earliest recollections of my adventurous childhood is the ride I had on a pony's side. I was passive in the whole matter. A little girl cousin of mine was put in a bag and suspended from the horn of an Indian saddle; but her weight had to be balanced or the saddle would not remain on the animal's back. Accordingly, I was put into another sack and made to keep the saddle and the girl in position! I did not object at all, for I had a very pleasant game of peek-a-boo with the little girl, until we came to a big snow-drift, where the poor beast was stuck fast and began to lie down. Then it was not so nice!

This was the convenient and primitive way in which some mothers packed their children for winter journeys. However cold the weather might be, the inmate of the fur-lined sack was usually very comfortable—at least I used to think so. I believe I was accustomed to all the precarious Indian conveyances, and, as a boy, I enjoyed the dog-travaux ride as much as any. The travaux consisted of a set of rawhide strips securely lashed to the tent-poles, which were harnessed to the sides of the animal as if he stood between shafts, while the free ends were allowed to drag on the ground. Both ponies and large dogs were used as beasts of burden, and they carried in this way the smaller children as well as the baggage.

This mode of traveling for children was possible only in the summer, and as the dogs were sometimes unreliable, the little ones were exposed to a certain amount of danger. For instance, whenever a train of dogs had been traveling for a long time, almost perishing with the heat and their heavy loads, a glimpse of water would cause them to forget all their responsibilities. Some of them, in spite of the screams of the women, would swim with their burdens into the cooling stream, and I was thus, on more than one occasion, made to partake of an unwilling bath.

I was a little over four years old at the time of the "Sioux massacre" in Minnesota. In the general turmoil, we took flight into British Columbia, and the journey is still vividly remembered by all our family. A yoke of oxen and a lumber-wagon were taken from some white farmer and brought home for our conveyance.

How delighted I was when I learned that we were to ride behind those wise-looking animals and in that gorgeously painted wagon! It seemed almost like a living creature to me, this new vehicle with four legs, and the more so when we got out of axle-grease and the wheels went along squealing like pigs!

The boys found a great deal of innocent fun in jumping from the high wagon while the oxen were leisurely moving along. My elder brothers soon became experts. At last, I mustered up courage enough to join them in this sport. I was sure they stepped on the wheel, so I cautiously placed my moccasined foot upon it. Alas! before I could realize what had happened, I was under the wheels, and had it not been for the neighbor immediately behind us, I might have been run over by the next team as well.

This was my first experience with a civilized vehicle. I cried out all possible reproaches on the white man's team and concluded that a dog travaux was good enough for me. I was really rejoiced that we were moving away from the people who made the wagon that had almost ended my life, and it did not occur to me that I alone was to blame. I could not be persuaded to ride in that wagon again and was glad when we finally left it beside the Missouri river.

The summer after the "Minnesota massacre," General Sibley pursued our people across this river. Now the Missouri is considered one of the most treacherous rivers in the world. Even a good modern boat is not safe upon its uncertain current. We were forced to cross in buffalo-skin boats—as round as tubs!

The *Washechu* (white men) were coming in great numbers with their big guns, and while most of our men were fighting them to gain time, the women and the old men made and equipped the temporary boats, braced with ribs of willow. Some of these were towed by two or three women or men swimming in the water and some by ponies. It was not an easy matter to keep them right side up, with their helpless freight of little children and such goods as we possessed.

In our flight, we little folks were strapped in the saddles or held in front of an older person, and in the long night marches to get away from the soldiers, we suffered from loss of sleep and insufficient food. Our meals were eaten hastily, and sometimes in the saddle. Water was not always to be found. The people carried it with them in bags formed of tripe or the dried pericardium of animals.

Now we were compelled to trespass upon the country of hostile tribes and were harassed by them almost daily and nightly. Only the strictest vigilance saved us.

One day we met with another enemy near the British lines. It was a prairie fire. We were surrounded. Another fire was quickly made, which saved our lives.

One of the most thrilling experiences of the following winter was a blizzard, which overtook us in our wanderings. Here and there, a family lay down in the snow, selecting a place where it was not likely to drift much. For a day and a night we lay under the snow. Uncle stuck a long pole beside us to tell us when the storm was over. We had plenty of buffalo robes and the snow kept us warm, but we found it heavy. After a time, it became packed and hollowed out around our bodies, so that we were as comfortable as one can be under those circumstances.

The next day the storm ceased, and we discovered a large herd of buffaloes almost upon us. We dug our way out, shot some of the buffaloes, made a fire and enjoyed a good dinner.

I was now an exile as well as motherless; yet I was not unhappy. Our wanderings from place to place afforded us many pleasant experiences and quite as many hardships and misfortunes. There were times of plenty and times of scarcity, and we had several narrow escapes from death. In savage life, the early spring is the most trying time and almost all the famines occurred at this period of the year.

The Indians are a patient and a clannish people; their love for one another is stronger than that of any civilized people I know. . . .

In times of famine, the adults often denied themselves in order to make the food last as long as possible for the children, who were not able to bear hunger as well as the old. As a people, they can live without food much longer than any other nation.

I once passed through one of these hard springs when we had nothing to eat for several days. I well remember the six small birds which constituted the breakfast for six families one morning; and then we had no dinner or supper to follow! What a relief that was to me—although I had only a small wing of a small bird for my share! Soon after this, we came into a region where buffaloes were plenty, and hunger and scarcity were forgotten.

Such was the Indian's wild life! When game was to be had and the sun shone, they easily forgot the bitter experiences of the winter before. Little preparation was made for the future. They are children of Nature, and occasionally she whips them with the lashes of experience, yet they are forgetful and careless. Much of their suffering might have been prevented by a little calculation.

During the summer, when Nature is at her best, and provides abundantly for the savage, it seems to me that no life is happier than his! Food is free—lodging free—everything free! All were alike rich in the summer, and, again, all were alike poor in the winter and early spring. However, their diseases were fewer and not so destructive as now, and the

Indian's health was generally good. The Indian boy enjoyed such a life as almost all boys dream of and would choose for themselves if they were permitted to do so.

The raids made upon our people by other tribes were frequent, and we had to be constantly on the watch. I remember at one time a night attack was made upon our camp and all our ponies stampeded. Only a few of them were recovered, and our journeys after this misfortune were effected mostly by means of the dog-travaux.

The second winter after the massacre, my father and my two older brothers, with several others, were betrayed by a half-breed at Winnipeg to the United States authorities. As I was then living with my uncle in another part of the country, I became separated from them for ten years. During all this time we believed that they had been killed by the whites, and I was taught that I must avenge their deaths as soon as I was able to go upon the war-path.

I must say a word in regard to the character of this uncle, my father's brother, who was my adviser and teacher for many years. He was a man about six feet two inches in height, very erect and broad-shouldered. He was known at that time as one of the best hunters and bravest warriors among the Sioux in British America, where he still lives, for to this day we have failed to persuade him to return to the United States.

He is a typical Indian—not handsome, but truthful and brave. He had a few simple principles from which he hardly ever departed. Some of these I shall describe when I speak of my early training.

It is wonderful that any children grew up through all the exposures and hardships that we suffered in those days! The frail teepee pitched anywhere, in the winter as well as in the summer, was all the protection that we had against cold and storms. I can recall times when we were snowed in and it was very difficult to get fuel. We were once three days without much fire and all of this time it stormed violently. There seemed to be no special anxiety on the part of our people;

they rather looked upon all this as a matter of course, knowing that the storm would cease when the time came.

I could once endure as much cold and hunger as any of them; but now if I miss one meal or accidentally wet my feet, I feel it as much as if I had never lived in the manner I have described, when it was a matter of course to get myself soaking wet many a time. Even if there was plenty to eat, it was thought better for us to practice fasting sometimes; and hard exercise was kept up continually, both for the sake of health and to prepare the body for the extraordinary exertions that it might, at any moment, be required to undergo. In my own remembrance, my uncle used often to bring home a deer on his shoulder. The distance was sometimes considerable; yet he did not consider it any sort of a feat.

The usual custom with us was to eat only two meals a day and these were served at each end of the day. This rule was not invariable, however, for if there should be any callers, it was Indian etiquette to offer either tobacco or food, or both. The rule of two meals a day was more closely observed by the men—especially the younger men—than by the women and children. This was when the Indians recognized that a true manhood, one of physical activity and endurance, depends upon dieting and regular exercise. No such system is practiced by the reservation Indians of today.

My Indian Grandmother

As a motherless child, I always regarded my good grandmother as the wisest of guides and the best of protectors. It was not long before I began to realize her superiority to most of her contemporaries. This idea was not gained entirely from my own observation, but also from a knowledge of the high regard in which she was held by other women. Aside from her native talent and ingenuity, she was endowed with a truly wonderful memory. No other midwife in her day and tribe could compete with her in skill and judgment. Her observations in practice were all preserved in her mind for reference, as systematically as if they had been written upon the pages of a note-book.

I distinctly recall one occasion when she took me with her into the woods in search of certain medicinal roots.

"Why do you not use all kinds of roots for medicines?" said I.

"Because," she replied, in her quick, characteristic manner, "the Great Mystery does not will us to find things too easily. In that case everybody would be a medicine-giver, and Ohiyesa must learn that there are many secrets which the Great Mystery will disclose only to the most worthy. Only those who seek him fasting and in solitude will receive his signs."

With this and many similar explanations she wrought in my soul wonderful and lively conceptions of the "Great Mystery" and of the effects of prayer and solitude. I continued my childish questioning.

"But why did you not dig those plants that we saw in the woods, of the same kind that you are digging now?"

"For the same reason that we do not like the berries we find in the shadow of deep woods as well as the ones which grow in sunny places. The latter have more sweetness and flavor. Those herbs which have medicinal virtues should be sought in a place that is neither too wet nor too dry, and where they have a generous amount of sunshine to maintain their vigor.

"Some day Ohiyesa will be old enough to know the secrets of medicine; then I will tell him all. But if you should grow up to be a bad man, I must withhold these treasures from you and give them to your brother, for a medicine man must be a good and wise man. I hope Ohiyesa will be a great medicine man when he grows up. To be a great warrior is a noble ambition; but to be a mighty medicine man is a nobler!"

She said these things so thoughtfully and impressively that I cannot but feel and remember them even to this day.

Our native women gathered all the wild rice, roots, berries and fruits which formed an important part of our food. This was distinctively a woman's work. Uncheedah (grandmother) understood these matters perfectly, and it became a kind of instinct with her to know just where to look for each edible variety and at what season of the year. This sort of labor gave the Indian women every opportunity to observe and study Nature after their fashion; and in this Uncheedah was more acute than most of the men. The abilities of her boys were not all inherited from their father; indeed, the stronger family traits came obviously from her. She was a leader among the native women, and they came to her, not only for medical aid, but for advice in all their affairs.

In bravery she equaled any of the men. This trait, together with her ingenuity and alertness of mind, more than once saved her and her people from destruction. Once, when we were roaming over a region occupied by other tribes, and on a day when most of the men were out upon the hunt, a party of hostile Indians suddenly appeared. Although there were a few men left at home, they were taken by surprise at first and scarcely knew what to do, when this woman came forward and advanced alone to meet our foes. She had gone some distance when some of the men followed her. She met the strangers and offered her hand to them. They accepted her friendly greeting; and as a result of her brave act we were left unmolested and at peace. . . .

The Indian women, after reaching middle age, are usually heavy and lack agility, but my grandmother was in this also an exception. She was fully sixty when I was born; and when I was seven years old she swam across a swift and wide stream, carrying me on her back, because she did not wish to expose me to accident in one of the clumsy round boats of bull-hide which were rigged up to cross the rivers which impeded our way, especially in the springtime. Her strength and endurance were remarkable. Even after she had attained the age of eighty-two, she one day walked twenty-five miles without appearing much fatigued.

I marvel now at the purity and elevated sentiment possessed by this woman, when I consider the customs and habits of her people at the time. When her husband died she was still comparatively a young woman—still active, clever and industrious. She was descended from a haughty chieftain of the "Dwellers among the Leaves." Although women of her age and position were held to be eligible to re-marriage, and she had several persistent suitors who were men of her own age and chiefs, yet she preferred to cherish in solitude the memory of her husband.

I was very small when my uncle brought home two Ojibway young women. In the fight in which they were captured, none of the Sioux war party had been killed; therefore they were sympathized with and tenderly treated by the Sioux women. They were apparently happy, although of course they felt deeply the losses sustained at the time of their capture, and they did not fail to show their appreciation of the kindnesses received at our hands.

As I recall now the remarks made by one of them at the time of their final release, they appear to me quite remarkable. They lived in my grandmother's family for two years, and were then returned to their people at a great peace council of the two nations. When they were about to leave my grandmother, the elder of the two sisters first embraced her, and then spoke somewhat as follows:

"You are a brave woman and a true mother. I understand now why your son so bravely conquered our band, and took my sister and myself captive. I hated him at first, but now I admire him, because he did just what my father, my brother or my husband would have done had they opportunity. He did even more. He saved us from the tomahawks of his fellow-warriors, and brought us to his home to know a noble and a brave woman.

"I shall never forget your many favors shown to us. But I must go. I belong to my tribe and I shall return to them. I will endeavor to be a true woman also, and to teach my boys to be generous warriors like your son."

Her sister chose to remain among the Sioux all her life, and she married one of our young men.

"I shall make the Sioux and the Ojibways," she said, "to be as brothers."

There are many other instances of intermarriage with captive women. The mother of the well-known Sioux chieftain, Wabashaw, was an Ojibway woman. I once knew a woman who was said to be a white captive. She was married to a noted warrior, and had a fine family of five boys. She was well accustomed to the Indian ways, and as a child I should not have suspected that she was white. The skins of these people became so sunburned and full of paint that it required a keen eye to distinguish them from the real Indians.

An Indian Sugar Camp

With the first March thaw the thoughts of the Indian women of my childhood days turned promptly to the annual sugar-making. This industry was chiefly followed by the old men and women and the children. The rest of the tribe went out upon the spring fur-hunt at this season, leaving us at home to make the sugar.

The first and most important of the necessary utensils were the huge iron and brass kettles for boiling. Everything else could be made, but these must be bought, begged or borrowed. A maple tree was felled and a log canoe hollowed out, into which the sap was to be gathered. Little troughs of basswood and birchen basins were also made to receive the sweet drops as they trickled from the tree.

As soon as these labors were accomplished, we all proceeded to the bark sugar house, which stood in the midst of a fine grove of maples on the bank of the Minnesota river. We found this hut partially filled with the snows of winter and the withered leaves of the preceding autumn, and it must be cleared for our use. In the meantime a tent was pitched outside for a few days' occupancy. The snow was still deep in the woods, with a solid crust upon which we could easily walk; for we usually moved to the sugar house before the sap had actually started, the better to complete our preparations.

My grandmother worked like a beaver in these days (or rather like a muskrat, as the Indians say; for this industrious little animal sometimes collects as many as six or eight bushels of edible roots for the winter, only to be robbed of his store by some of our people). If there was prospect of a good sugaring season, she now made a second and even a third canoe to contain the sap. These canoes were afterward utilized by the hunters for their proper purpose. . . .

Presently the weather moderated and the snow began to melt. The month of April brought showers which carried most of the snow off into the Minnesota river. Now the women began to test the trees—moving leisurely among them, axe in hand, and striking a single quick blow, to see if the sap would appear. The trees, like people, have their individual characters; some were ready to yield up their life-blood, while others were more reluctant. Now one of the birchen basins was set under each tree, and a hardwood chip driven deep into the cut which the axe had made. From the corners of this chip—at first drop by drop, then more freely—the sap trickled into the little dishes. . . .

A long fire was now made in the sugar house, and a row of brass kettles suspended over the blaze. The sap was collected by the women in tin or birchen buckets and poured into the canoes, from which the kettles were kept filled. The hearts of the boys beat high with pleasant anticipations when they heard the welcome hissing sound of the boiling sap! Each boy claimed one kettle for his especial charge. It was his duty to see that the fire was kept up under it, to watch lest it boil over, and finally, when the sap became syrup, to test it upon the snow, dipping it out with a wooden paddle. So frequent were these tests that for the first day or two we consumed nearly all that could be made; and it was not until the sweetness began to pall that my grandmother set herself in earnest to store up sugar for future use. She made it into cakes of various forms, in birchen molds, and sometimes in hollow canes or reeds, and the bills of ducks and geese. Some of it was pulverized and packed in rawhide cases. Being a prudent woman, she did not give it to us after the first month or so, except upon special occasions, and it was thus made to last almost the year around. The smaller candies were reserved as an occasional treat for the little fellows, and the sugar was eaten at feasts with wild rice or parched corn, and also with pounded dried meat. Coffee and tea, with their substitutes, were all unknown to us in those days. . . .

I remember the occasion of our last sugar bush in Minnesota, that I stood one day outside of our hut and watched the approach of a visitor—a bent old man, his hair almost white, and carrying on his back a large bundle of red willow, or *kinnikinick*, which the Indians use for smoking. He threw down his load at the door and thus saluted us: "You have indeed perfect weather for sugar-making."

It was my great-grandfather, Cloud Man, whose original village was on the shores of Lakes Calhoun and Harriet, now in the suburbs of the city of Minneapolis. He was the first Sioux chief to welcome the Protestant missionaries among his people, and a well-known character in those pioneer days. . . .

A Midsummer Feast

It was midsummer. Everything that the Santee Sioux had undertaken during the year had been unusually successful. The spring fur-hunters had been fortunate, and the heavy winter had proved productive of much maple sugar. The women's patches of maize and potatoes were already sufficiently advanced to use. The *Wahpetonwan* band of Sioux, the "Dwellers among the Leaves," were fully awakened to the fact that it was almost time for the midsummer festivities of the old, wild days.

The invitations were bundles of tobacco, and acceptances were sent back from the various bands—the "Light Lodges", "Dwellers back from the River," and many others, in similar fashion. Blue Earth, chief of the "Dwellers among the Leaves," was the host.

There were to be many different kinds of athletic games; indeed, the festival was something like a State fair, in that there were many side shows and competitive events. For instance, supposing that (Miss) White Rabbit should desire to give a "maidens' feast," she would employ a crier to go among the different bands announcing the fact in a sing-song manner:

"Miss White Rabbit will receive her maiden friends today at noon, inside of the circular encampment of the *Kaposia* band."

Again, should (Mr.) Sleepy Eye wish to have his child's ears pierced publicly, he would have to give away a great deal of savage wealth—namely, otter, bear and beaver skins and ponies—or the child would not be considered as belonging to a family in good standing.

But the one all-important event of the occasion was the lacrosse game, for which it had been customary to select those two bands which could boast the greater number of fast runners.

The *Wahpetonwan* village on the banks of the Minnesota river was alive with the newly-arrived guests and the preparations for the coming event. Meat of wild game had been put away with much care during the previous fall in anticipation of this feast. There was wild rice and the choicest of dried venison that had been kept all winter, as well as freshly dug turnips, ripe berries and an abundance of fresh meat.

Along the edge of the woods the teepees were pitched in groups or semi-circles, each band distinct from the others. The teepee of Mankato or Blue Earth was pitched in a conspicuous spot. Just over the entrance was painted in red and yellow a picture of a pipe, and directly opposite this the rising sun. The painting was symbolic of welcome and good will to men under the bright sun.

A meeting was held to appoint some "medicine man" to make the balls that were to be used in the lacrosse contest; and presently the herald announced that this honor had been conferred upon old Chankpee-yuhah, or "Keeps the Club," while every other man of his profession was disappointed. He was a powerful man physically, who had apparently won the confidence of the people by his fine personal appearance and by working upon superstitious minds.

Towards evening he appeared in the circle, leading by the hand a boy about four years old. Closely the little fellow observed every motion of the man; nothing escaped his vigilant black eyes, which seemed constantly to grow brighter and larger, while his exuberant glossy black hair was plaited and wound around his head like that of a Celestial. He wore a bit of swan's down in each ear, which formed a striking contrast with the child's complexion. Further than this, the boy was painted according to the fashion of the age. He held in his hands a miniature bow and arrows.

The medicine man drew himself up in an admirable attitude, and proceeded to make his short speech:

"*Wahpetonwans*, you boast that you run down the elk; you can outrun the Ojibways. Before you all, I dedicate to you this red ball. *Kaposias*, you claim that no one has a lighter foot than you; you declare that you can endure running a whole day without water. To you I dedicate this black ball. Either you or the Leaf-Dwellers will have to drop your eyes and bow your head when the game is over. I wish to announce that if the *Wahpetonwans* should win, this little warrior shall bear the name Ohiyesa (winner) through life; but if the Light Lodges should win, let the name be given to any child appointed by them."

The ground selected for the great final game was on a narrow strip of land between a lake and the river. It was about three quarters of a mile long and a quarter of a mile in width. The spectators had already ranged themselves all along the two sides, as well as at the two ends, which were somewhat higher than the middle. The soldiers appointed to keep order furnished much of the entertainment of the day. They painted artistically and tastefully, according to the Indian fashion, not only their bodies but also their ponies and clubs. They were so strict in enforcing the laws that no one could venture with safety within a few feet of the limits of the field. . . .

The most powerful men were stationed at the half-way ground, while the fast runners were assigned to the back. It was an impressive spectacle—a fine collection of agile forms, almost stripped of garments and painted in wild imitation of the rainbow and sunset sky on human canvas. Some had undertaken to depict the Milky Way across their tawny bodies, and one or two made a bold attempt to reproduce the lightning. Others contented themselves with painting the figure of some fleet animal or swift bird on their muscular chests.

The coiffure of the Sioux lacrosse player has often been unconsciously imitated by the fashionable hair-dressers of modern times. Some banged and singed their hair; others did a little more by adding powder. The Grecian knot was located on the wrong side of the head, being tied tightly over the forehead. A great many simply brushed back their long locks and tied them with a strip of otter skin.

At the middle of the ground were stationed four immense men, magnificently formed. A fifth approached this group, paused a moment, and then threw his head back, gazed up into the sky in the manner of a cock and gave a smooth, clear operatic tone. Instantly the little black ball went up between the two middle rushers, in the midst of yells, cheers and war-whoops. Both men endeavored to catch it in the air; but alas! each interfered with the other; then the guards on each side rushed upon them. For a time, a hundred lacrosse sticks vied with each other, and the wriggling human flesh and paint were all one could see through the cloud of dust. Suddenly there shot swiftly through the air toward the south, toward the *Kaposias'* goal, the ball. There was a general cheer from their adherents, which echoed back from the white cliff on the opposite side of the Minnesota.

As the ball flew through the air, two adversaries were ready to receive it. The *Kaposia* quickly met the ball, but failed to catch it in his netted bag, for the other had swung his up like a flash. Thus it struck the ground, but had no opportunity to bound up when a *Wahpeton* pounced upon it like a cat and slipped out of the grasp of his opponents. A mighty cheer thundered through the air.

The warrior who had undertaken to pilot the little sphere was risking much, for he must dodge a host of *Kaposias* before he could gain any ground. He was alert and agile; now springing like a panther, now leaping like a deer over a stooping opponent who tried to seize him around the waist. Every opposing player was upon his heels, while those of his own side did all in their power to clear the way for him. But it was all in vain. He only gained fifty paces.

Thus the game went. First one side, then the other would gain an advantage, and then it was lost, until the herald proclaimed that it was time to change the ball. No victory was in sight for either side. . . .

The ball had not been allowed to come to the surface since it reached this point, for there were more than a hundred men who scrambled for it. Suddenly a warrior shot out of the throng like the ball itself! Then some of the players shouted: "Look out for Antelope! Look out for Antelope!" But it was too late. The little sphere had already nestled into Antelope's palm and that fleetest of *Wahpetons* had thrown down his lacrosse stick and set a determined eye upon the northern goal.

Such a speed! He had cleared almost all the opponents' guards—there were but two more. These were exceptional runners of the *Kaposias*. As he approached them in his almost irresistible speed, every savage heart thumped louder in the Indian's dusky bosom. In another moment there would be a defeat for the *Kaposias* or a prolongation of the game. The two men, with a determined look approached their foe like two panthers prepared to spring; yet he neither slackened his speed nor deviated from his course. A crash—a mighty shout!—the two *Kaposias* collided, and the swift Antelope had won the laurels!

The turmoil and commotion at the victors' camp were indescribable. A few beats of a drum were heard, after which the criers hurried along the lines, announcing the last act to be performed at the camp of the "Leaf Dwellers."

The day had been a perfect one. Every event had been a success; and, as a matter of course, the old people were happy, for they largely profited by these occasions. Within the circle formed by the general assembly sat in a group the members of the common council. Blue Earth arose, and in a few appropriate and courteous remarks assured his guests that it was not selfishness that led his braves to carry off the honors of the last event, but that this was a friendly contest in which each band must assert its prowess. In memory of this victory, the boy would now receive his name. A loud "Ho-o-o" of approbation reverberated from the edge of the forest upon the Minnesota's bank.

Half frightened, the little fellow was now brought into the circle, looking very much as if he were about to be executed. Cheer after cheer went up for the awe-stricken boy. Chankpee-yuhah, the medicine man, proceeded to confer the name.

"Ohiyesa (or Winner) shall be thy name hence-forth. Be brave, be patient and thou shalt always win! Thy name is Ohiyesa."

An Indian Boy's Training

It is commonly supposed that there is no systematic education of their children among the aborigines of this country. Nothing could be farther from the truth. All the customs of this primitive people were held to be divinely instituted, and those in connection with the training of children were scrupulously adhered to and transmitted from one generation to another.

The expectant parents conjointly bent all their efforts to the task of giving the new-comer the best they could gather from a long line of ancestors. A pregnant Indian woman would often choose one of the greatest characters of her family and tribe as a model for her child. This hero was daily called to mind. She would gather from tradition all of his noted deeds and daring exploits, rehearsing them to herself when alone. In order that the impression might be more distinct, she avoided company. She isolated herself as much as possible, and wandered in solitude, not thoughtlessly, but with an eye to the impress given by grand and beautiful scenery.

The Indians believed, also, that certain kinds of animals would confer peculiar gifts upon the unborn, while others would leave so strong an adverse impression that the child might become a monstrosity. A case of hare-lip was commonly attributed to the rabbit. It was said that a rabbit had charmed the mother and given to the babe its own features. Even the meat of certain animals was denied the pregnant woman, because it was supposed to influence the disposition or features of the child.

Scarcely was the embryo warrior ushered into the world, when he was met by lullabies that speak of wonderful exploits in hunting and war. Those ideas which so fully occupied his mother's mind before his birth are now put into words by all about the child, who is as yet quite unresponsive to their appeals to his honor and ambition. He is called the future defender of his people, whose lives may depend upon his courage and skill. If the child is a girl, she is at once addressed as the future mother of a noble race.

In hunting songs, the leading animals are introduced; they come to the boy to offer their bodies for the sustenance of his tribe. The animals are regarded as his friends, and spoken of almost as tribes of people, or as his cousins, grandfathers and grandmothers. The songs of wooing, adapted as lullabies, were equally imaginative, and the suitors were often animals personified, while pretty maidens were represented by the mink and the doe.

Very early, the Indian boy assumed the task of preserving and transmitting the legends of his ancestors and his race. Almost every evening a myth, or a true story of some deed done in the past, was narrated by one of the parents or grandparents, while the boy listened with parted lips and glistening eyes. On the following evening, he was usually required to repeat it. If he was not an apt scholar, he struggled long with his task; but, as a rule, the Indian boy is a good listener and has a good memory, so that the stories were tolerably well mastered. The household became his audience, by which he was alternately criticized and applauded.

This sort of teaching at once enlightens the boy's mind and stimulates his ambition. His conception of his own future career becomes a vivid and irresistible force. Whatever there is for him to learn must be learned; whatever qualifications are necessary to a truly great man he must seek at any expense of danger and hardship. Such was the feeling of the imaginative and brave young Indian. It became apparent to him in early life that he must accustom himself to rove alone and not to fear or dislike the impression of solitude.

It seems to be a popular idea that all the characteristic skill of the Indian is instinctive and hereditary. This is a mistake. All the stoicism and patience of the Indian are acquired traits, and continual practice alone makes him master of the art of wood-craft. Physical training and dieting were not neg-

lected. I remember that I was not allowed to have beef soup
or any warm drink. The soup was for the old men. General
rules for the young were never to take their food very hot,
nor to drink much water.

My uncle, who educated me up to the age of fifteen years,
was a strict disciplinarian and a good teacher. When I left the
teepee in the morning, he would say: "Hakadah, look closely
to everything you see"; and at evening, on my return, he used
often to catechize me for an hour or so.

"On which side of the trees is the lighter-colored bark? On
which side do they have most regular branches?"

It was his custom to let me name all the new birds that I
had seen during the day. I would name them according to the
color or the shape of the bill or their song or the appearance
and locality of the nest—in fact, anything about the bird that
impressed me as characteristic. I made many ridiculous
errors, I must admit. He then usually informed me of the correct name. Occasionally I made a hit and this he would warm-
ly commend.

He went much deeper into this science when I was a little
older, that is, about the age of eight or nine years. He would
say, for instance:

"How do you know that there are fish in yonder lake?"

"Because they jump out of the water for flies at mid-day."

He would smile at my prompt but superficial reply.

"What do you think of the little pebbles grouped together under the shallow water? And, what made the pretty
curved marks in the sandy bottom and the little sand-banks?
Where do you find the fish-eating birds? Have the inlet and
the outlet of a lake anything to do with the question?"

He did not expect a correct reply at once to all the volu-
minous questions that he put to me on these occasions, but
he meant to make me observant and a good student of
nature.

"Hakadah," he would say to me, "you ought to follow the
example of the *shunktokecha* (wolf). Even when he is surprised

and runs for his life, he will pause to take one more look at you before he enters his final retreat. So you must take a second look at everything you see.

"It is better to view animals unobserved. I have been a witness to their courtships and their quarrels and have learned many of their secrets in this way. I was once the unseen spectator of a thrilling battle between a pair of grizzly bears and three buffaloes—a rash act for the bears, for it was in the moon of strawberries, when the buffaloes sharpen and polish their horns for bloody contests among themselves.

"I advise you, my boy, never to approach a grizzly's den from the front, but to steal up behind and throw your blanket or a stone in front of the hole. He does not usually rush for it, but first puts his head out and listens and then comes out very indifferently and sits on his haunches on the mound in front of the hole before he makes any attack. While he is exposing himself in this fashion, aim at his heart. Always be as cool as the animal himself." Thus he armed me against the cunning of savage beasts by teaching me how to outwit them.

"In hunting," he would resume, "you will be guided by the habits of the animal you seek. Remember that a moose stays in swampy or low land or between high mountains near a spring or lake, for thirty to sixty days at a time. Most large game moves about continually, except the doe in the spring; it is then a very easy matter to find her with the fawn. Conceal yourself in a convenient place as soon as you observe any signs of the presence of either, and then call with your birchen doe-caller.

"Whichever one hears you first will soon appear in your neighborhood. But you must be very watchful, or you may be made a fawn of by a large wild-cat. They understand the characteristic call of the doe perfectly well.

"When you have any difficulty with a bear or a wild-cat—that is, if the creature shows signs of attacking you—you must make him fully understand that you have seen him and are aware of his intentions. If you are not well equipped for a pitched battle, the only way to make him retreat is to take a long sharp-pointed pole for a spear and rush toward him. No wild beast will face this unless he is cornered and already wounded. These fierce beasts are generally afraid of the common weapon of the larger animals—the horns, and if these are very long and sharp, they dare not risk an open fight.

"There is one exception to this rule—the grey wolf will attack fiercely when very hungry. But their courage depends upon their numbers; in this they are like white men. One wolf or two will never attack a man. They will stampede a herd of buffaloes in order to get at the calves; they will rush upon a herd of antelopes, for these are helpless; but they are always careful about attacking man."

Of this nature were the instructions of my uncle, who was widely known at that time as among the greatest hunters of his tribe.

All boys were expected to endure hardship without complaint. In savage warfare, a young man must, of course, be an athlete and used to undergoing all sorts of privations. He must be able to go without food and water for two or three days without displaying any weakness, or to run for a day and a night without any rest. He must be able to traverse a pathless and wild country without losing his way either in the day or night time. He cannot refuse to do any of these things if he aspires to be a warrior.

Sometimes my uncle would waken me very early in the morning and challenge me to fast with him all day. I had to accept the challenge. We blackened our faces with charcoal, so that every boy in the village would know that I was fasting for the day. Then the little tempters would make my life a misery until the merciful sun hid behind the western hills.

I can scarcely recall the time when my stern teacher began to give sudden war-whoops over my head in the morning while I was sound asleep. He expected me to leap up with perfect presence of mind, always ready to grasp a weapon of some sort and to give a shrill whoop in reply. If I was sleepy or startled and hardly knew what I was about, he would ridicule me and say that I need never expect to sell my scalp dear. Often he would vary these tactics by shooting off his gun just outside of the lodge while I was yet asleep, at the same time giving blood-curdling yells. After a time I became used to this.

When Indians went upon the war-path, it was their custom to try the new warriors thoroughly before coming to an engagement. For instance, when they were near a hostile camp, they would select the novices to go after the water and make them do all sorts of things to prove their courage. In accordance with this idea, my uncle used to send me off after water when we camped after dark in a strange place. Perhaps the country was full of wild beasts, and, for aught I knew, there might be scouts from hostile bands of Indians lurking in that very neighborhood.

Yet I never objected, for that would show cowardice. I picked my way through the woods, dipped my pail in the water and hurried back, always careful to make as little noise as a cat. Being only a boy, my heart would leap at every crackling of a dry twig or distant hooting of an owl, until, at last, I reached our teepee. Then my uncle would perhaps say: "Ah, Hakadah, you are a thorough warrior," empty out the precious contents of the pail, and order me to go a second time.

Imagine how I felt! But I wished to be a brave man as much as a white boy desires to be a great lawyer or even President of the United States. Silently I would take the pail and endeavor to retrace my footsteps in the dark.

With all this, our manners and morals were not neglected. I was made to respect the adults and especially the aged. I was not allowed to join in their discussions, nor even to speak in their presence, unless requested to do so. Indian etiquette was very strict, and among the requirements was that of avoiding the direct address. A term of relationship or some title of courtesy was commonly used instead of the personal name by those who wished to show respect. We were taught generosity to the poor and reverence for the "Great Mystery." Religion was the basis of all Indian training.

I recall to the present day some of the kind warnings and reproofs that my good grandmother was wont to give me. "Be strong of heart—be patient!" she used to say. She told me of a young chief who was noted for his uncontrollable temper. While in one of his rages he attempted to kill a woman, for which he was slain by his own band and left unburied as a mark of disgrace—his body was simply covered with green grass. If I ever lost my temper, she would say:

"Hakadah, control yourself, or you will be like that young man I told you of, and lie under a green blanket!"

In the old days, no young man was allowed to use tobacco in any form until he had become an acknowledged warrior and had achieved a record. If a youth should seek a wife before he had reached the age of twenty-two or twenty-three, and been recognized as a brave man, he was sneered at and considered an ill-bred Indian. He must also be a skillful hunter. An Indian cannot be a good husband unless he brings home plenty of game.

These precepts were in the line of our training for the wild life.

My Plays and Playmates

Games and Sports

The Indian boy was a prince of the wilderness. He had but very little work to do during the period of his boyhood. His principal occupation was the practice of a few simple arts in warfare and the chase. Aside from this, he was master of his time.

Whatever was required of us boys was quickly performed: then the field was clear for our games and plays. There was always keen competition among us. We felt very much as our fathers did in hunting and war—each one strove to excel all the others.

It is true that our savage life was a precarious one, and full of dreadful catastrophes; however, this never prevented us from enjoying our sports to the fullest extent. As we left our teepees in the morning, we were never sure that our scalps would not dangle from a pole in the afternoon!

It was an uncertain life, to be sure. Yet we observed that the fawns skipped and played happily while the gray wolves might be peeping forth from behind the hills, ready to tear them limb from limb.

Our sports were molded by the life and customs of our people; indeed, we practiced only what we expected to do when grown. Our games were feats with the bow and arrow, foot and pony races, wrestling, swimming and imitation of the customs and habits of our fathers. We had sham fights with mud balls and willow wands; we played lacrosse, made war upon bees, shot winter arrows (which were used only in that season), and coasted upon the ribs of animals and buffalo robes.

No sooner did the boys get together than, as a usual thing, they divided into squads and chose sides; then a leading arrow was shot at random into the air. Before it fell to the ground a volley from the bows of the participants followed. Each player was quick to note the direction and speed of the leading arrow and he tried to send his own at the same speed and at an equal height, so that when it fell it would be closer to the first than any of the others.

It was considered out of place to shoot by first sighting the object aimed at. This was usually impracticable in actual life, because the object was almost always in motion, while the hunter himself was often upon the back of a pony at full gallop. Therefore, it was the off-hand shot that the Indian boy sought to master. There was another game with arrows that was characterized by gambling, and was generally confined to the men.

The races were an every-day occurrence. At noon the boys were usually gathered by some pleasant sheet of water and as soon as the ponies were watered, they were allowed to graze for an hour or two, while the boys stripped for their noonday sports. A boy might say to some other whom he considered his equal:

"I can't run; but I will challenge you to fifty paces."

A former hero, when beaten, would often explain his defeat by saying: "I drank too much water."

Boys of all ages were paired for a "spin," and the little red men cheered on their favorites with spirit.

As soon as this was ended, the pony races followed. All the speedy ponies were picked out and riders chosen. If a boy declined to ride, there would be shouts of derision.

Last of all came the swimming. A little urchin would hang to his pony's long tail, while the latter, with only his head above water, glided sportively along. Finally the animals were driven into a fine field of grass and we turned our attention to other games.

Lacrosse was an older game and was confined entirely to the Sisseton and Santee Sioux. Shinny, such as is enjoyed by white boys on the ice, is still played on the open prairie by the western Sioux. The "moccasin game," although sometimes played by the boys, was intended mainly for adults. . . .

Wrestling was largely indulged in by us all. It may seem odd, but wrestling was done by a great many boys at once— from ten to any number on a side. It was really a battle, in which each one chose his opponent. The rule was that if a boy sat down, he was let alone, but as long as he remained standing within the field, he was open to an attack. No one struck with the hand, but all manner of tripping with legs and feet and butting with the knees was allowed. Altogether it was an exhausting pastime—fully equal to the American game of football and only the young athlete could really enjoy it.

One of our most curious sports was a war upon the nests of wild bees. We imagined ourselves about to make an attack upon the Ojibways or some tribal foe. We all painted ourselves and stole cautiously upon the nest; then, with a rush and war whoop, sprang upon the object of our attack and endeavored to destroy it. But it seemed that the bees were always on the alert and never entirely surprised, for they always raised quite as many scalps as did their bold assailants! After the onslaught upon the nest was ended, we usually followed it by a pretended scalp dance. . . .

We had some quiet plays which we alternated with the more severe and warlike ones. Among them were throwing wands and snow-arrows. In the winter we coasted much. We had no "double-rippers" or toboggans, but six or seven of the long ribs of a buffalo, fastened together at the larger end, answered all practical purposes. Sometimes a strip of basswood bark, four feet long and about six inches wide, was used with considerable skill. We stood on one end and held the other, using the slippery inside of the bark for the outside, and thus coasting down long hills with remarkable speed.

The spinning of tops was one of the all-absorbing winter sports. We made our tops heart shaped of wood, horn or bone. We whipped them with a long thong of buckskin. The handle was a stick about a foot long and sometimes we whittled the stick to make it spoon-shaped at one end.

We played games with these tops—two to fifty boys at one time. Each whips his top until it hums; then one takes the lead and the rest follow in a sort of obstacle race. The top must spin all the way through. There were bars of snow over which we must pilot our top in the spoon end of our whip; then again we would toss it in the air on to another open spot of ice or smooth snow-crust from twenty to fifty paces away. The top that holds out the longest is the winner.

Sometimes we played "medicine dance." This, to us, was almost what "playing church" is among white children, but our people seemed to think it an act of irreverence to imitate these dances, therefore performances of this kind were always enjoyed in secret. We used to observe all the important

ceremonies and it required something of an actor to reproduce the dramatic features of the dance. The real dances
occupied a day and a night, and the program was long and
varied, so that it was not easy to execute all the details perfectly; but the Indian children are born imitators.

The boys built an arbor of pine boughs in some out-of-
the-way place and at one end of it was a rude lodge. This was
the medicine lodge or headquarters. All the initiates were
there. At the further end or entrance were the door-keepers
or soldiers, as we called them. The members of each lodge
entered in a body, standing in single file and facing the headquarters. Each stretched out his right hand and a prayer was
offered by the leader, after which they took the places
assigned to them.

When the preliminaries had been completed, our leader
sounded the big drum and we all said "A-ho-ho-ho!" as a sort
of amen. Then the choir began their song and whenever they
ended a verse, we all said again "A-ho-ho-ho!" At last they
struck up the chorus and we all got upon our feet and began
to dance, by simply lifting up one foot and then the other,
with a slight swing to the body.

Each boy was representing or imitating some one of the
medicine men. We painted and decorated ourselves just as
they did and carried bird or squirrel skins, or occasionally live
birds and chipmunks as our medicine bags and small white
shells or pebbles for medicine charms.

Then the persons to be initiated were brought in and seated, with much ceremony, upon a blanket or buffalo robe.
Directly in front of them the ground was leveled smooth and
here we laid an old pipe filled with dried leaves for tobacco.
Around it we placed the variously colored feathers of the
birds we had killed, and cedar and sweet-grass we burned for
incense.

Finally those of us who had been selected to perform this
ceremony stretched out our arms at full length, holding the
sacred medicine bags and aiming them at the new members.

After swinging them four times, we shot them suddenly forward, but did not let go. The novices then fell forward on their faces as if dead. Quickly a chorus was struck up and we all joined in a lively dance around the supposed bodies. The girls covered them up with their blankets, thus burying the dead. At last we resurrected them with our charms and led them to their places among the audience. Then came the last general dance and the final feast.

I was often selected as choir-master on these occasions, for I had happened to learn many of the medicine songs and was quite an apt mimic. My grandmother, who was a noted medicine woman of the Turtle lodge, on hearing of these sacrilegious acts (as she called them) warned me that if any of the medicine men should discover them, they would punish me terribly by shriveling my limbs with slow disease. . . .

When we played "hunting buffalo" we would send a few good runners off on the open prairie with a supply of meat; then start a few equally swift boys to chase them and capture the food. Once we were engaged in this sport when a real hunt by the men was in progress; yet we did not realize that it was so near until, in the midst of our play, we saw an immense buffalo coming at full speed directly toward us. Our mimic buffalo hunt turned into a very real buffalo scare. Fortunately, we were near the edge of the woods and we soon disappeared among the leaves like a covey of young prairie-chickens and some hid in the bushes while others took refuge in tall trees.

We loved to play in the water. When we had no ponies, we often had swimming matches of our own and sometimes made rafts with which we crossed lakes and rivers. It was a common thing to "duck" a young or timid boy or to carry him into deep water to struggle as best he might.

I remember a perilous ride with a companion on an unmanageable log, when we were both less than seven years old. The older boys had put us on this uncertain bark and pushed us out into the swift current of the river. I cannot speak for my comrade in distress, but I can say now that I would rather ride on a swift bronco any day than try to stay on and steady a short log in a river. I never knew how we managed to prevent a shipwreck on that voyage and to reach the shore.

We had many curious wild pets. There were young foxes, bears, wolves, raccoons, fawns, buffalo calves and birds of all kinds, tamed by various boys. My pets were different at different times, but I particularly remember one. I once had a grizzly bear for a pet and so far as he and I were concerned, our relations were charming and very close. But I hardly know whether he made more enemies for me or I for him. It was his habit to treat every boy or his conduct in my interest and I was hated on account of his interference.

My Playmates

Chatanna was the brother with whom I passed much of my early childhood. From the time that I was old enough to play with boys, this brother was my close companion. He was a handsome boy, and an affectionate comrade. We played together, slept together and ate together; and as Chatanna was three years the older, I naturally looked up to him as to a superior.

Oesedah was a beautiful little character. She was my cousin, and four years younger than myself. Perhaps none of my early playmates are more vividly remembered than is this little maiden.

The name given her by a noted medicine-man was Makah-oesetopah-win. It means The-four-corners-of-the-earth. As she was rather small, the abbreviation with a diminutive termination was considered more appropriate, hence Oesedah became her common name.

Although she had a very good mother, Uncheedah was her efficient teacher and chaperon.

Such knowledge as my grandmother deemed suitable to a maiden was duly impressed upon her susceptible mind.

When I was not in the woods with Chatanna, Oesedah was my companion at home; and when I returned from my play at evening, she would have a hundred questions ready for me to answer. Some of these were questions concerning our every-day life, and others were more difficult problems which had suddenly dawned upon her active little mind. Whatever had occurred to interest her during the day was immediately repeated for my benefit.

There were certain questions upon which Oesedah held me to be authority, and asked with the hope of increasing her little store of knowledge. I have often heard her declare to her girl companions: "I know it is true; Ohiyesa said so!" Uncheedah was partly responsible for this, for when any questions came up which lay within the sphere of man's observation, she would say:

"Ohiyesa ought to know that: he is a man—I am not! You had better ask him."

The truth was that she had herself explained to me many of the subjects under discussion.

I was occasionally referred to little Oesedah in the same manner, and I always accepted her childish elucidations of any matter upon which I had been advised to consult her, because I knew the source of her wisdom. In this simple way we were made to be teachers of one another. . . .

At another time, when I was engaged in a similar discussion with my brother Chatanna, Oesedah came to my rescue. Our grandmother had asked us:

"What bird shows most judgment in caring for its young?"

Chatanna at once exclaimed:

"The eagle!" but I held my peace for a moment, because I was confused—so many birds came into my mind at once. I finally declared:

"It is the oriole!"

Chatanna was asked to state all the evidence that he had in support of the eagle's good sense in rearing its young. He proceeded with an air of confidence:

"The eagle is the wisest of all birds. Its nest is made in the safest possible place, upon a high and inaccessible cliff. It provides its young with an abundance of fresh meat. They have the freshest of air. They are brought up under the spell of the grandest scenes, and inspired with lofty feelings and bravery. They see that all other beings live beneath them, and that they are the children of the King of Birds. A young eagle shows the spirit of a warrior while still in the nest.

"Being exposed to the inclemency of the weather the young eaglets are hardy. They are accustomed to hear the mutterings of the Thunder Bird and the sighings of the Great Mystery. Why, the little eagles cannot help being as noble as they are, because their parents selected for them so lofty and inspiring a home! How happy they must be when they find themselves above the clouds, and behold the zigzag flashes of lightning all about them! It must be nice to taste a piece of fresh meat up in their cool home, in the burning summertime! Then when they drop down the bones of the game they feed upon, wolves and vultures gather beneath them, feeding upon their refuse. That alone would show them their chieftainship over all the other birds. Isn't that so, grandmother?" Thus triumphantly he concluded his argument.

I was staggered at first by the noble speech of Chatannna, but I soon recovered from its effects. The little Oesedah came to my aid by saying: "Wait until Ohiyesa tells of the loveliness of the beautiful Oriole's home!" This timely remark gave me courage and I began:

"My grandmother, who was it said that a mother who has a gentle and sweet voice will have children of a good disposition? I think the oriole is that kind of a parent. It provides both sunshine and shadow for its young. Its nest is suspended from the prettiest bough of the most graceful tree, where it is rocked by the gentle winds; and the one we found yesterday was beautifully lined with soft things, both deep and warm, so that the little featherless birdies cannot suffer from the cold and wet."

Here Chatanna interrupted me to exclaim: "That is just like the white people—who cares for them? The eagle teaches its young to be accustomed to hardships, like young warriors!"

Ohiyesa was provoked; he reproached his brother and appealed to the judge, saying that he had not finished yet.

"But you would not have lived, Chatanna, if you had been exposed like that when you were a baby! The oriole shows wisdom in providing for its children a good, comfortable home! A home upon a high rock would not be pleasant—it would be cold! We climbed a mountain once, and it was cold there; and who would care to stay in such a place when it storms? What wisdom is there in having a pile of rough sticks upon a bare rock, surrounded with ill-smelling bones of animals, for a home? Also, my uncle says that the eaglets seem always to be on the point of starvation. You have heard that whoever lives on game killed by some one else is compared to an eagle. Isn't that so, grandmother?

"The oriole suspends its nest from the lower side of a horizontal bough so that no enemy can approach it. It enjoys peace and beauty and safety."

Oesedah was at Ohiyesa's side during the discussion, and occasionally whispered into his ear. Uncheedah decided this time in favor of Ohiyesa. . . .

My little cousin and I went to school together in later years; but she could not endure the confinement of the school-room. Although apparently very happy, she suffered greatly from the change to an indoor life, as have many of our people, and died six months after our return to the United States.

The Boy Hunter

It will be no exaggeration to say that the life of the Indian hunter was a life of fascination. From the moment that he lost sight of his rude home in the midst of the forest, his untutored mind lost itself in the myriad beauties and forces of nature. Yet he never forgot his personal danger from some lurking foe or savage beast, however absorbing was his passion for the chase.

The Indian youth was a born hunter. Every motion, every step expressed an inborn dignity and, at the same time, a depth of native caution. His moccasined foot fell like the velvet paw of a cat—noiselessly; his glittering black eyes scanned every object that appeared within their view. Not a bird, not even a chipmunk, escaped their piercing glance.

I was scarcely over three years old when I stood one morning just outside our buffalo-skin teepee, with my little bow and arrows in my hand, and gazed up among the trees. Suddenly the instinct to chase and kill seized me powerfully. Just then a bird flew over my head and then another caught my eye, as it balanced itself upon a swaying bough. Everything else was forgotten and in that moment I had taken my first step as a hunter.

There was almost as much difference between the Indian boys who were brought up on the open prairies and those of the woods, as between city and country boys. The hunting of the prairie boys was limited and their knowledge of natural history imperfect. They were, as a rule, good riders, but in all-round physical development much inferior to the red men of the forest.

Our hunting varied with the season of the year, and the nature of the country which was for the time our home. Our chief weapon was the bow and arrows, and perhaps, if we were lucky, a knife was possessed by some one in the crowd. In the olden times, knives and hatchets were made from bone and sharp stones.

For fire we used a flint with a spongy piece of dry wood and a stone to strike with. Another way of starting fire was for several of the boys to sit down in a circle and rub two pieces of dry, spongy wood together, one after another, until the wood took fire.

We hunted in company a great deal, though it was a common thing for a boy to set out for the woods quite alone, and he usually enjoyed himself fully as much. Our game consisted mainly of small birds, rabbits, squirrels and grouse. Fishing, too, occupied much of our time. We hardly ever passed a creek or a pond without searching for some signs of fish. When fish were present, we always managed to get some. Fish-lines were made of wild hemp, sinew or horse-hair. We either caught fish with lines, snared or speared them, or shot them with bow and arrows. In the fall we charmed them up to the surface by gently tickling them with a stick and quickly threw them out. We have sometimes dammed the brooks and driven the larger fish into a willow basket made for that purpose.

It was part of our hunting to find new and strange things in the woods. We examined the slightest sign of life; and if a bird had scratched the leaves off the ground, or a bear dragged up a root for his morning meal, we stopped to speculate on the time it was done. If we saw a large old tree with some scratches on its bark, we concluded that a bear or some raccoons must be living there. In that case we did not go any nearer than was necessary, but later reported the incident at home. An old deer-track would at once bring on a warm discussion as to whether it was the track of a buck or a doe. Generally, at noon, we met and compared our game, noting at the same time the peculiar characteristics of everything we had killed. It was not merely a hunt, for we combined with it the study of animal life. We also kept strict account of our game, and thus learned who were the best shots among the boys. . . .

We used to climb large trees for birds of all kinds; but we never undertook to get young owls unless they were on the ground. The hooting owl especially is a dangerous bird to attack under these circumstances. I was once trying to catch a yellow-winged wood-pecker in its nest when my arm became twisted and lodged in the deep hole so that I could not get it out without the aid of a knife; but we were a long way from home and my only companion was a deaf mute cousin of mine. I was about fifty feet up in the tree, in a very uncomfortable position, but I had to wait there for more than an hour before he brought me the knife with which I finally released myself.

Our devices for trapping small animals were rude, but they were often successful. For instance, we used to gather up a peck or so of large, sharp pointed burrs and scatter them in the rabbit's furrow-like path. In the morning, we would find the little fellow sitting quietly in his tracks, unable to move, for the burrs stuck to his feet.

Another way of snaring rabbits and grouse was the following: We made nooses of twisted horsehair, which we tied very firmly to the top of a limber young tree, then bent the latter down to the track and fastened the whole with a slip-knot, after adjusting the noose. When the rabbit runs his head through the noose, he pulls the slip-knot and is quickly carried up by the spring of the young tree. This is a good plan, for the rabbit is out of harm's way as he swings high in the air.

Perhaps the most enjoyable of all was the chipmunk hunt. We killed these animals at any time of year, but the special time to hunt them was in March. After the first thaw, the chipmunks burrow a hole through the snow crust and make their first appearance for the season. Sometimes as many as fifty will come together and hold a social reunion. These gatherings occur early in the morning, from daybreak to about nine o'clock.

We boys learned this, among other secrets of nature, and got our blunt-headed arrows together in good season for the chipmunk expedition.

We generally went in groups of six to a dozen or fifteen, to see which would get the most. On the evening before, we selected several boys who could imitate the chipmunk's call with wild oat straws and each of these provided himself with a supply of straws.

The crust will hold the boys nicely at this time of the year. Bright and early, they all come together at the appointed place, from which each group starts out in a different direction, agreeing to meet somewhere at a given position of the sun.

My first experience of this kind is still well remembered. It was a fine crisp March morning, and the sun had not yet shown himself among the distant tree-tops as we hurried along through the ghostly wood. Presently we arrived at a place where there were many signs of the animals. Then each of us selected a tree and took up his position behind it. The chipmunk caller sat upon a log as motionless as he could, and began to call.

Soon we heard the patter of little feet on the hard snow; then we saw the chipmunks approaching from all directions. Some stopped and ran experimentally up a tree or a log, as if uncertain of the exact direction of the call; others chased one another about.

In a few minutes, the chipmunk-caller was besieged with them. Some ran all over his person, others under him and still others ran up the tree against which he was sitting. Each boy remained immovable until their leader gave the signal; then a great shout arose, and the chipmunks in their flight all ran up the different trees.

Now the shooting-match began. The little creatures seemed to realize their hopeless position; they would try again and again to come down the trees and flee away from the deadly aim of the youthful hunters. But they were shot down very fast; and whenever several of them rushed toward the ground, the little red-skin hugged the tree and yelled frantically to scare them up again.

Each boy shoots always against the trunk of the tree, so that the arrow may bound back to him every time; otherwise, when he had shot away all of them, he would be helpless, and another, who had cleared his own tree, would come and take away his game, so there was warm competition. Sometimes a desperate chipmunk would jump from the top of the tree in order to escape, which was considered a joke on the boy who lost it and a triumph for the brave little animal. At last all were killed or gone, and then we went on to another place, keeping up the sport until the sun came out and the chipmunks refused to answer the call. . . .

It became a necessary part of our education to learn to prepare a meal while out hunting. It is a fact that most Indians will eat the liver and some other portions of large animals raw, but they do not eat fish or birds uncooked. Neither will they eat a frog, or an eel. On our boyish hunts, we often went on until we found ourselves a long way from our camp, when we would kindle a fire and roast a part of our game.

Generally we broiled our meat over the coals on a stick. We roasted some of it over the open fire. But the best way to cook fish and birds is in the ashes, under a big fire. We take the fish fresh from the creek or lake, have a good fire on the sand, dig in the sandy ashes and bury it deep. The same thing is done in case of a bird, only we wet the feathers first. When it is done, the scales or feathers and skin are stripped off whole, and the delicious meat retains all its juices and flavor. We pulled it off as we ate, leaving the bones undisturbed.

Our people had also a method of boiling without pots or kettles. A large piece of tripe was thoroughly washed and the ends tied, then suspended between four stakes driven into the ground and filled with cold water. The meat was then placed in this novel receptacle and boiled by means of the addition of red-hot stones. . . .

Hakadah's First Offering

"Hakadah, *coowah!*" was the sonorous call that came from a large teepee in the midst of the Indian encampment. In answer to the summons there emerged from the woods, which were only a few steps away, a boy, accompanied by a splendid black dog. There was little in the appearance of the little fellow to distinguish him from the other Sioux boys.

He hastened to the tent from which he had been summoned, carrying in his hands a bow and arrows gorgeously painted, while the small birds and squirrels that he had killed with these weapons dangled from his belt.

Within the tent sat two old women, one on each side of the fire. Uncheedah was the boy's grandmother, who had brought up the motherless child. Wahchewin was only a caller, but she had been invited to remain and assist in the first personal offering of Hakadah to the "Great Mystery."

This was a matter which had, for several days, pretty much monopolized Uncheedah's mind. It was her custom to see to this when each of her children attained the age of eight summers. They had all been celebrated as warriors and hunters among their tribe, and she had not hesitated to claim for herself a good share of the honors they had achieved, because she had brought them early to the notice of the "Great Mystery."

She believed that her influence had helped to regulate and develop the characters of her sons to the height of savage nobility and strength of manhood.

It had been whispered through the teepee village that Uncheedah intended to give a feast in honor of her grandchild's first sacrificial offering. This was mere speculation, however, for the clear-sighted old woman had determined to keep this part of the matter secret until the offering should be completed, believing that the "Great Mystery" should be met in silence and dignity.

The boy came rushing into the lodge, followed by his dog Ohitika who was wagging his tail promiscuously, as if to say: "Master and I are really hunters!"

Hakadah breathlessly gave a descriptive narrative of the killing of each bird and squirrel as he pulled them off his belt and threw them before his grandmother.

"This blunt-headed arrow," said he, "actually had eyes this morning. Before the squirrel can dodge around the tree it strikes him in the head, and, as he falls to the ground, my Ohitika is upon him."

He knelt upon one knee as he talked, his black eyes shining like evening stars.

"Sit down here," said Uncheedah to the boy; "I have something to say to you. You see that you are now almost a man. Observe the game you have brought me! It will not be long before you will leave me, for a warrior must seek opportunities to make him great among his people.

"You must endeavor to equal your father. and grandfather," she went on. "They were warriors and feast-makers. But it is not the poor hunter who makes many feasts. Do you not remember the 'Legend of the Feast-Maker,' who gave forty feasts in twelve moons? And have you forgotten the story of the warrior who sought the will of the Great Mystery? Today you will make your first offering to him."

The concluding sentence fairly dilated the eyes of the young hunter, for he felt that a great event was about to occur, in which he would be the principal actor. But Uncheedah resumed her speech.

"You must give up one of your belongings—whichever is dearest to you—for this is to be a sacrificial offering."

This somewhat confused the boy; not that he was selfish, but rather uncertain as to what would be the most appropriate thing to give. Then, too, he supposed that his grandmother referred to his ornaments and playthings only. So he volunteered:

"I can give up my best bow and arrows, and all the paints I have, and—and my bear's claws necklace, grandmother!"

"Are these the things dearest to you?" she demanded.

"Not the bow and arrows, but the paints will be very hard to get, for there are no white people near; and the necklace—it is not easy to get one like it again. I will also give up my otter-skin head-dress, if you think that is not enough."

111

"But think, my boy, you have not yet mentioned the thing that will be a pleasant offering to the Great Mystery."

The boy looked into the woman's face with a puzzled expression.

"I have nothing else as good as those things I have named, grandmother, unless it is my spotted pony; and I am sure that the Great Mystery will not require a little boy to make him so large a gift. Besides, my uncle gave three otter-skins and five eagle-feathers for him and I promised to keep him a long while, if the Blackfeet or the Crows do not steal him."

Uncheedah was not fully satisfied with the boy's free offerings. Perhaps it had not occurred to him what she really wanted. But Uncheedah knew where his affection was vested. His faithful dog, his pet and companion—Hakadah was almost inseparable from the loving beast.

She was sure that it would be difficult to obtain his consent to sacrifice the animal, but she ventured upon a final appeal.

"You must remember," she said, "that in this offering you will call upon him who looks at you from every creation. In the wind you hear him whisper to you. He gives his warwhoop in the thunder. He watches you by day with his eye, the sun; at night, he gazes upon your sleeping countenance through the moon. In short, it is the Mystery of Mysteries, who controls all things to whom you will make your first offering. By this act, you will ask him to grant to you what he has granted to few men. I know you wish to be a great warrior and hunter. I am not prepared to see my Hakadah show any cowardice, for the love of possessions is a woman's trait and not a brave's."

During this speech, the boy had been completely aroused to the spirit of manliness, and in his excitement was willing to give up anything he had—even his pony! But he was unmindful of his friend and companion, Ohitika, the dog! So, scarcely had Uncheedah finished speaking, when he almost shouted:

"Grandmother, I will give up any of my possessions for the offering to the Great Mystery! You may select what you think will be most pleasing to him."

There were two silent spectators of this little dialogue. One was Wahchewin; the other was Ohitika. The woman had been invited to stay, although only a neighbor. The dog, by force of habit, had taken up his usual position by the side of his master when they entered the teepee. Without moving a muscle, save those of his eyes, he had been a very close observer of what passed.

Had the dog but moved once to attract the attention of his little friend, he might have been dissuaded from that impetuous exclamation: "Grandmother, I will give up any of my possessions!"

It was hard for Uncheedah to tell the boy that he must part with his dog, but she was equal to the situation.

"Hakadah," she proceeded cautiously, "you are a young brave. I know, though young, your heart is strong and your courage is great. You will be pleased to give up the dearest thing you have for your first offering. You must give up Ohitika. He is brave; and you, too, are brave. He will not fear death; you will bear his loss bravely. Come—here are four bundles of paints and a filled pipe—let us go to the place."

When the last words were uttered, Hakadah did not seem to hear them. He was simply unable to speak. To a civilized eye, he would have appeared at that moment like a little copper statue. His bright black eyes were fast melting in floods of tears, when he caught his grandmother's eye and recollected her oft-repeated adage: "Tears for woman and the war-whoop for man to drown sorrow!"

He swallowed two or three big mouthfuls of heart-ache and the little warrior was master of the situation.

"Grandmother, my Brave will have to die! Let me tie together two of the prettiest tails of the squirrels that he and I killed this morning, to show to the Great Mystery what a hunter he has been. Let me paint him myself."

This request Uncheedah could not refuse and she left the pair alone for a few minutes, while she went to ask Wacoota to execute Ohitika.

Every Indian boy knows that, when a warrior is about to meet death, he must sing a death dirge. Hakadah thought of his Ohitika as a person who would meet his death without a struggle, so he began to sing a dirge for him, at the same time hugging him tight to himself. As if he were a human being, he whispered in his ear:

"Be brave, my Ohitika! I shall remember you the first time I am upon the war-path in the Ojibway country."

At last he heard Uncheedah talking with a man outside the teepee, so he quickly took up his paints. Ohitika was a jet-black dog, with a silver tip on the end of his tail and on his nose, beside one white paw and a white star upon a protuberance between his ears. Hakadah knew that a man who prepares for death usually paints with red and black. Nature had partially provided Ohitika in this respect, so that only red was required and this Hakadah supplied generously.

Then he took off a piece of red cloth and tied it around the dog's neck; to this he fastened two of the squirrels' tails and a wing from the oriole they had killed that morning.

Just then it occurred to him that good warriors always mourn for their departed friends and the usual mourning was black paint. He loosened his black braided locks, ground a dead coal, mixed it with bear's oil and rubbed it on his entire face.

During this time every hole in the tent was occupied with an eye. Among the lookers-on was his grandmother. She was very near relenting. Had she not feared the wrath of the Great Mystery, she would have been happy to call out to the boy: "Keep your dear dog, my child!"

As it was, Hakadah came out of the teepee with his face looking like an eclipsed moon, leading his beautiful dog, who was even handsomer than ever with the red touches on his specks of white.

It was now Uncheedah's turn to struggle with the storm and burden in her soul. But the boy was emboldened by the people's admiration of his bravery, and did not shed a tear. As soon as she was able to speak, the loving grandmother said:

"No, my young brave, not so! You must not mourn for your first offering. Wash your face and then we will go."

The boy obeyed, submitted Ohitika to Wacoota with a smile, and walked off with his grandmother and Wahchewin.

They followed a well-beaten foot-path leading along the bank of the Assiniboine river, through a beautiful grove of oak, and finally around and under a very high cliff. The murmuring of the river came up from just below. On the opposite side was a perpendicular white cliff, from which extended back a gradual slope of land, clothed with the majestic mountain oak. The scene was impressive and wild.

Wahchewin had paused without a word when the little party reached the edge of the cliff. It had been arranged between her and Uncheedah that she should wait there for Wacoota, who was to bring as far as that the portion of the offering with which he had been entrusted.

The boy and his grandmother descended the bank, following a tortuous foot-path until they reached the water's edge. Then they proceeded to the mouth of an immense cave, some fifty feet above the river, under the cliff. A little stream of limpid water trickled down from a spring within the cave. The little watercourse served as a sort of natural staircase for the visitors. A cool, pleasant atmosphere exhaled from the mouth of the cavern. Really it was a shrine of nature and it is not strange that it was so regarded by the tribe.

A feeling of awe and reverence came to the boy. "It is the home of the Great Mystery," he thought to himself; and the impressiveness of his surroundings made him forget his sorrow.

Very soon Wahchewin came with some difficulty to the steps. She placed the body of Ohitika upon the ground in a life-like position and again left the two alone.

As soon as she disappeared from view, Uncheedah, with all solemnity and reverence, unfastened the leather strings that held the four small bundles of paints and one of tobacco, while the filled pipe was laid beside the dead Ohitika.

She scattered paints and tobacco all about. Again they stood a few moments silently; then she drew a deep breath and began her prayer to the Great Mystery:

"0, Great Mystery, we hear thy voice in the rushing waters below us! We hear thy whisper in the great oaks above! Our spirits are refreshed with thy breath from within this cave. 0, hear our prayer! Behold this little boy and bless him! Make him a warrior and a hunter as great as thou didst make his father and grandfather."

And with this prayer the little warrior had completed his first offering. . . .

Evening in the Lodge

Evening in the Lodge

I had been skating on that part of the lake where there was an overflow, and came home somewhat cold. I cannot say just how cold it was, but it must have been intensely so, for the trees were cracking all about me like pistol shots. I did not mind, because I was wrapped up in my buffalo robe with the hair inside, and a wide leather belt held it about my loins. My skates were nothing more than strips of basswood bark bound upon my feet.

I had taken off my frozen moccasins and put on dry ones in their places.

"Where have you been and what have you been doing?" Uncheedah asked as she placed before me some roast venison in a wooden bowl. "Did you see any tracks of moose or bear?"

"No, grandmother, I have only been playing at the lower end of the lake. I have something to ask you," I said, eating

Charles Eastman in traditional clothing.

Eastman in 1890, when he took his Medical Degree at Boston University.

Eastman at Knox College, 1880.

Photographs from the Life of Charles Eastman (Ohiyesa)

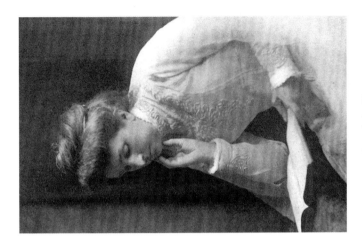

Elaine Goodale Eastman.

Many Lightnings. English name, Jacob Eastman. From an old daguerreotype of Dr. Eastman's father.

Eastman teaching archery at Camp Oahe.

Pine Ridge Agency, 1890.

Photographs from the Life of Charles Eastman (Ohiyesa)

Eastman and Stanley Johnson, a classmate at Dartmouth, at their 40th reunion in 1927.

Courtesy of Walter P. Reuther Library, Wayne State University.

Charles Eastman (Ohiyesa) at age 69.

Eastman with guide and bark canoe, on Rainy Lake, Ontario.

Eastman in 1916.

my dinner and supper together with all the relish of a hungry boy who has been skating in the cold for half a day.

"I found this feather, grandmother, and I could not make out what tribe wear feathers in that shape."

"Ugh, I am not a man; you had better ask your uncle. Besides, you should know it yourself by this time. You are now old enough to think about eagle feathers."

I felt mortified by this reminder of my ignorance. It seemed a reflection on me that I was not ambitious enough to have found all such matters out before.

"Uncle, you will tell me, won't you?" I said, in an appealing tone.

"I am surprised, my boy, that you should fail to recognize this feather. It is a Cree medicine feather, and not a warrior's."

"Then," I said, with much embarrassment, you had better tell me again, uncle, the language of the feathers. I have really forgotten it all."

The day was now gone; the moon had risen; but the cold had not lessened, for the trunks of the trees were still snapping all around our teepee, which was lighted and warmed by the immense logs which Uncheedah's industry had provided.

My uncle, White Foot-print, now undertook to explain to me the significance of the eagle's feather.

"The eagle is the most war-like bird," he began, "and the most kingly of all birds; besides, his feathers are unlike any others, and these are the reasons why they are used by our people to signify deeds of bravery.

"It is not true that when a man wears a feather bonnet, each one of the feathers represents the killing of a foe or even a coup. When a man wears an eagle feather upright upon his head, he is supposed to have counted one of four coups upon his enemy."

"Well, then, a coup does not mean the killing of an enemy?"

"No, it is the after-stroke or touching of the body after he falls. It is so ordered, because oftentimes the touching of an enemy is much more difficult to accomplish than the shooting of one from a distance. It requires a strong heart to face the whole body of the enemy, in order to count the coup on the fallen one, who lies under cover of his kinsmen's fire. Many a brave man has been lost in the attempt.

"When a warrior approaches his foe, dead or alive, he calls upon the other warriors to witness by saying: 'I, Fearless Bear, your brave, again perform the brave deed of counting the first (or second or third or fourth) coup upon the body of the bravest of your enemies.' Naturally, those who are present will see the act and be able to testify to it. When they return, the heralds, as you know, announce publicly all such deeds of valor, which then become a part of the man's war record. Any brave who would wear the eagle's feather must give proof of his right to do so.

"When a brave is wounded in the same battle where he counted his coup, he wears the feather hanging downward. When he is wounded, but makes no count, he trims his feather and in that case, it need not be an eagle feather. All other feathers are merely ornaments. When a warrior wears a feather with a round mark, it means that he slew his enemy. When the mark is cut into the feather and painted red, it means that he took the scalp.

"A brave who has been successful in ten battles is entitled to a war-bonnet; and if he is a recognized leader, he is permitted to wear one with long, trailing plumes. Also those who have counted many coups may tip the ends of the feathers with bits of white or colored down. Sometimes the eagle feather is tipped with a strip of weasel skin; that means the wearer had the honor of killing, scalping and counting the first coup upon the enemy all at the same time.

"This feather you have found was worn by a Cree—it is indiscriminately painted. All other feathers worn by the common Indians mean nothing," he added.

"Tell me, uncle, whether it would be proper for me to wear any feathers at all if I have never gone upon the war-path."

"You could wear any other kind of feathers, but not an eagle's," replied my uncle, "although sometimes one is worn on great occasions by the child of a noted man, to indicate the father's dignity and position.". . .

Adventures of My Uncle

It was a beautiful fall day—"a gopher's last look back," as we used to say of the last warm days of the late autumn. We were encamped beside a wild rice lake, where two months before we had harvested our watery fields of grain, and where we had now returned for the duck-hunting. All was well with us. Ducks were killed in countless numbers, and in the evenings the men hunted deer in canoes by torchlight along the shores of the lake. But alas! life is made up of good times and bad times, and it is when we are perfectly happy that we should expect some overwhelming misfortune.

"So it was that upon this peaceful and still morning, all of a sudden a harsh and terrible war-cry was heard! Your father was then quite a young man, and a very ambitious warrior, so that I was always frightened on his account whenever there was a chance of fighting. But I did not think of your uncle, Mysterious Medicine, for he was not over fifteen at the time; besides, he had never shown any taste for the field.

"Our camp was thrown into great excitement; and as the warriors advanced to meet the enemy, I was almost overcome by the sight of your uncle among them! It was of no use for me to call him back—I think I prayed in that moment to the Great Mystery to bring my boy safely home.

"I shall never forget, as long as I live, the events of that day. Many brave men were killed; among them two of your uncle's intimate friends. But when the battle was over, my boy came back; only his face was blackened in mourning for his

119

friends, and he bore several wounds in his body. I knew that he had proved himself a true warrior.

"This was the beginning of your uncle's career, He has surpassed your father and your grandfather; yes, all his ancestors except Jingling Thunder, in daring and skill."

Such was my grandmother's account of the maiden battle of her third son, Mysterious Medicine. He achieved many other names; among them Big Hunter, Long Rifle and White Footprint.

He had a favorite Kentucky rifle which he carried for many years. The stock was several times broken, but he always made another. With this gun he excelled most of his contemporaries in accuracy of aim. He used to call the weapon *Ishtahbopopa*—a literal translation would be "Pops-the-eye."

My uncle, who was a father to me for ten years of my life, was almost a giant in his proportions, very symmetrical and "straight as an arrow." His face was not at all handsome. He had very quiet and reserved manners and was a man of action rather than of unnecessary words. Behind the veil of Indian reticence he had an inexhaustible fund of wit and humor; but this part of his character only appeared before his family and very intimate friends. Few men know nature more thoroughly than he. Nothing irritated him more than to hear some natural fact misrepresented. . . .

He was always modest and unconscious of self in relating his adventures. "I have often been forced to realize my danger," he used to say, "but not in such a way as to overwhelm me. Only twice in my life have I been really frightened, and for an instant lost my presence of mind. . . . *(His first lengthy adventure has been deleted.)*

"The other time was on the plains, in summer. I was accustomed to hunting in the woods, and never before had hunted buffalo on horseback. Being a young man, of course I was eager to do whatever other men did. Therefore I saddled my pony for the hunt. I had a swift pony and a good gun, but on this occasion I preferred a bow and arrows.

"It was the time of year when the buffalo go in large herds and the bulls are vicious. But this did not trouble me at all; indeed, I thought of nothing but the excitement and honor of the chase.

"A vast plain near the Souris river was literally covered with an immense herd. The day was fair, and we came up with them very easily. I had a quiver full of arrows, with a sinew-backed bow.

"My pony carried me in far ahead of all the others. I found myself in the midst of the bulls first, for they are slow. They threw toward me vicious glances, so I hastened my pony on to the cows. Soon I was enveloped in a thick cloud of dust, and completely surrounded by the herd, who were by this time in the act of fleeing, their hoofs making a noise like thunder.

"I could not think of anything but my own situation, which confused me for the moment. It seemed to me to be a desperate one. If my pony, which was going at full speed, should step into a badger hole, I should be thrown to the ground and trampled under foot in an instant. If I were to stop, they would knock me over, pony and all. Again, it seemed as if my horse must fall from sheer exhaustion; and then what would become of me?

"At last I awoke to a calm realization of my own power. I uttered a yell and began to shoot right and left. Very soon there were only a few old bulls who remained near me. The herd had scattered, and I was miles away from my companions.

"It is when we think of our personal danger that we are apt to be at a loss to do the best thing under the circumstances. One should be unconscious of self in order to do his duty. We are very apt to think ourselves brave, when we are most timid. I have discovered that half our young men give the war-whoop when they are frightened, because they fear lest their silence may betray their state of mind. I think we are really bravest when most calm and slow to action.". . .

The Maiden's Feast

There were many peculiar customs among the Indians of an earlier period, some of which tended to strengthen the character of the people and preserve their purity. Perhaps the most unique of these was the annual "feast of maidens." The casual observer would scarcely understand the full force and meaning of this ceremony.

The last one that I ever witnessed was given at Fort Ellis, Manitoba, about the year 1871. Upon the table land just back of the old trading post and fully a thousand feet above the Assiniboine river, surrounded by groves, there was a natural amphitheatre. At one end stood the old fort where since 1830 the northern tribes had come to replenish their powder horns and lead sacks and to dispose of their pelts.

In this spot there was a reunion of all the renegade Sioux on the one hand and of the Assiniboines and Crees, the Canadian tribes, on the other. They were friendly. The matter was not formally arranged, but it was usual for all the tribes to meet here in the month of July. . . .

When circumstances are favorable, the Indians are the happiest people in the world. There were entertainments every single day, which everybody had the fullest opportunity to see and enjoy. If anything, the poorest profited the most by these occasions, because a feature in each case was the giving away of savage wealth to the needy in honor of the event. At any public affair, involving the pride and honor of a prominent family, there must always be a distribution of valuable presents.

One bright summer morning, while we were still at our meal of jerked buffalo meat, we heard the herald of the *Wahpeton* band upon his calico pony as he rode around our circle.

"White Eagle's daughter, the maiden Red Star, invites all the maidens of all the tribes to come and partake of her feast. It will be in the *Wahpeton* camp, before the sun reaches the middle of the sky. All pure maidens are invited. Red Star also invites the young men to be present, to see that no unworthy maiden should join in the feast."

The herald soon completed the rounds of the different camps, and it was not long before the girls began to gather in great numbers. The fort was fully alive to the interest of these savage entertainments. This particular feast was looked upon as a semi-sacred affair. It would be desecration for any to attend who was not perfectly virtuous. Hence it was regarded as an opportune time for the young men to satisfy themselves as to who were the virtuous maids of the tribe.

There were apt to be surprises before the end of the day. Any young man was permitted to challenge any maiden whom he knew to be unworthy. But woe to him who could not prove his case. It meant little short of death to the man who endeavored to disgrace a woman without cause.

The youths had a similar feast of their own, in which the eligibles were those who had never spoken to a girl in the way of courtship. It was considered ridiculous so to do before attaining some honor as a warrior, and the novices prided themselves greatly upon their self control.

From the various camps the girls came singly or in groups, dressed in bright-colored calicoes or in heavily fringed and beaded buckskin. Their smooth cheeks and the central part of their glossy hair was touched with vermilion. All brought with them wooden basins to eat from. Some who came from a considerable distance were mounted upon ponies; a few, for company or novelty's sake, rode double.

The maidens' circle was formed about a cone shaped rock which stood upon its base. This was painted red. Beside it two new arrows were lightly stuck into the ground. This is a sort of altar, to which each maiden comes before taking her assigned place in the circle, and lightly touches first the stone and then the arrows. By this oath she declares her purity. Whenever a girl approaches the altar there is a stir among the spectators, and sometimes a rude youth would call out:

"Take care! You will overturn the rock, or pull out the arrows!"

Such a remark makes the girls nervous, and especially one who is not sure of her composure. . . .

There was never a more gorgeous assembly of the kind than this one. The day was perfect. The Crees, displaying their characteristic horsemanship, came in groups; the Assiniboines, with their curious pompadour well covered with red paint. The various bands of Sioux all carefully observed the traditional peculiarities of dress and behavior. The attaches of the fort were fully represented at the entertainment, and it was not unusual to see a pale-face maiden take part in the feast.

The whole population of the region had assembled, and the maidens came shyly into the circle. The simple ceremonies observed prior to the serving of the food were in progress, when among a group of *Wahpeton* Sioux young men there was a stir of excitement. All the maidens glanced nervously toward the scene of the disturbance. Soon a tall youth emerged from the throng of spectators and advanced toward the circle. Every one of the chaperons glared at him as if to deter him from his purpose. But with a steady step he passed them by and approached the maidens' circle.

At last he stopped behind a pretty Assiniboine maiden of good family and said:

"I am sorry, but, according to custom, you should not be here."

The girl arose in confusion, but she soon recovered her self-control.

"What do you mean?" she demanded, indignantly. "Three times you have come to court me, but each time I have refused to listen to you. I turned my back upon you. Twice I was with Mashtinna. She can tell the people that this is true. The third time I had gone for water when you intercepted me and begged me to stop and listen. I refused because I did not know you. My chaperon, Makatopawee, knows that I was gone but a few minutes. I never saw you anywhere else."

The young man was unable to answer this unmistakable statement of facts, and it became apparent that he had sought to revenge himself for her repulse.

"Woo! woo! Carry him out!" was the order of the chief of the Indian police, and the audacious youth was hurried away into the nearest ravine to be chastised.

The young woman who had thus established her good name returned to the circle, and the feast was served. The "maidens' song" was sung, and four times they danced in a ring around the altar. Each maid as she departed once more took her oath to remain pure until she should meet her husband. . . .

Indian Life and Adventure

Life in the Woods

The month of September recalls to every Indian's mind the season of the fall hunt. I remember one such expedition which is typical of many. Our party appeared on the northwestern side of Turtle mountain; for we had been hunting buffaloes all summer, in the region of the Mouse river, between that mountain and the upper Missouri.

As our cone-shaped teepees rose in clusters along the outskirts of the heavy forest that clothes the sloping side of the mountain, the scene below was gratifying to a savage eye. The rolling yellow plains were checkered with herds of buffaloes. Along the banks of the streams that ran down from the mountains were also many elk, which usually appear at morning and evening, and disappear into the forest during the warmer part of the day. Deer, too, were plenty, and the brooks were alive with trout. Here and there the streams were dammed by the industrious beaver.

In the interior of the forest there were lakes with many islands, where moose, elk, deer and bears were abundant. The water-fowl were wont to gather here in great numbers, among them the crane, the swan, the loon, and many of the smaller kinds. The forest also was filled with a great variety of birds. Here the partridge drummed his loudest, while the whippoorwill sang with spirit, and the hooting owl reigned in the night.

To me, as a boy, this wilderness was a paradise. It was a land of plenty. To be sure, we did not have any of the luxuries of civilization, but we had every convenience and opportunity and luxury of Nature. We had also the gift of enjoying our good fortune, whatever dangers might lurk about us; and the truth is that we lived in blessed ignorance of any life that was better than our own.

As soon as hunting in the woods began, the customs regulating it were established. The council teepee no longer existed. A hunting bonfire was kindled every morning at daybreak, at which each brave must appear and report. The man who failed to do this before the party set out on the day's hunt was harassed by ridicule. As a rule, the hunters started before sunrise, and the brave who was announced throughout the camp as the first one to return with a deer on his back, was a man to be envied.

The legend-teller, old Smoky Day, was chosen herald of the camp, and it was he who made the announcements. After supper was ended, we heard his powerful voice resound among the teepees in the forest. He would then name a man to kindle the bonfire the next morning. His suit of fringed buckskin set off his splendid physique to advantage.

Scarcely had the men disappeared in the woods each morning than all the boys sallied forth, apparently engrossed in their games and sports, but in reality competing actively with one another in quickness of observation. As the day advanced, they all kept the sharpest possible lookout. Suddenly there would come the shrill "*Woo-coo-hoo!*" at the top of a boy's voice, announcing the bringing in of a deer. Immediately all the other boys took up the cry, each one bent on getting ahead of the rest. Now we all saw the brave Wacoota fairly bent over by his burden, a large deer which he carried on his shoulders. His fringed buckskin shirt was besprinkled with blood. He threw down the deer at the door of his wife's mother's home, according to custom, and then walked proudly to his own. At the door of his father's teepee he stood for a moment straight as a pine-tree, and then entered.

When a bear was brought in, a hundred or more of these urchins were wont to make the woods resound with their voices: "Wah! wah! wah! Wah! wah! wah! The brave White Rabbit brings a bear! Wah! wah! wah!"

All day these sing-song cheers were kept up, as the game was brought in. At last, toward the close of the afternoon, all the hunters had returned, and happiness and contentment reigned absolute, in a fashion which I have never observed among the white people, even in the best of circumstances. The men were lounging and smoking; the women actively engaged in the preparation of the evening meal, and the care of the meat. The choicest of the game was cooked and offered to the Great Mystery, with all the accompanying ceremonies. This we called the "medicine feast." Even the women, as they lowered the boiling pot, or the fragrant roast of venison ready to serve, would first whisper: "Great Mystery, do thou partake of this venison, and still be gracious!" This was the commonly said "grace."

Everything went smoothly with us, on this occasion, when we first entered the woods. Nothing was wanting to our old way of living. The killing of deer and elk and moose had to be stopped for a time, since meat was so abundant that we had no use for them any longer. Only the hunting for pelts, such as those of the bear, beaver, marten, and otter was continued. . . .

The leaves had now begun to fall, and the heavy frosts made the nights very cold. We were forced to realize that the short summer of that region had said adieu! Still we were gay and light-hearted, for we had plenty of provisions, and no misfortune had yet overtaken us in our wanderings over the country for nearly three months.

One day old Smoky Day returned from the daily hunt with an alarm. He had seen a sign—a "smoke sign." This had not appeared in the quarter that they were anxiously watching—it came from the east. After a long consultation among the men, it was concluded from the nature and duration of the smoke that it proceeded from an accidental fire. It was further surmised that the fire was not made by Sioux, since it was out of their country, but by a war-party of Ojibways, who were accustomed to use matches when lighting their pipes, and to throw them carelessly away. It was thought that a little time had been spent in an attempt to put it out.

The council decreed that a strict look-out should be established in behalf of our party. Every day a scout was appointed to reconnoitre in the direction of the smoke. It was agreed that no gun should be fired for twelve days. All our signals were freshly rehearsed among the men. The women and old men went so far as to dig little convenient holes around their lodges, for defense in case of a sudden attack. And yet an Ojibway scout would not have suspected, from the ordinary appearance of the camp, that the Sioux had become aware of their neighborhood! Scouts were stationed just outside of the village at night. They had been so trained as to rival an owl or a cat in their ability to see in the dark.

The twelve days passed by, however, without bringing any evidence of the nearness of the supposed Ojibway war-party, and the "lookout" established for purposes of protection was abandoned. Soon after this, one morning at dawn, we were aroused by the sound of the unwelcome war-whoop. Although only a child, I sprang up and was about to rush out, as I had been taught to do; but my good grandmother pulled me down, and gave me a sign to lay flat on the ground. I sharpened my ears and lay still.

All was quiet in camp, but at some little distance from us there was a lively encounter. I could distinctly hear the old herald, shouting and yelling in exasperation. "Whoo! whoo!" was the signal of distress, and I could almost hear the pulse of my own blood-vessels.

Closer and closer the struggle came, and still the women appeared to grow more and more calm. At last a tremendous charge by the Sioux put the enemy to flight; there was a burst of yelling; alas! my friend and teacher, old Smoky Day, was silent. He had been pierced to the heart by an arrow from the Ojibways.

Although successful, we had lost two of our men, Smoky Day and White Crane, and this incident, although hardly unexpected, darkened our peaceful sky. The camp was filled with songs of victory, mingled with the wailing of the relatives of the slain. . . .

(A lengthy description has been deleted of an unsuccessful war-party in which many young men were killed.) The first sad shock over, then came the change of habiliments. In savage usage, the outward expression of mourning surpasses that of civilization. The Indian mourner gives up all his good clothing, and contents himself with scanty and miserable garments. Blankets are cut in two, and the hair is cropped short. Often a devoted mother would scarify her arms or legs; a sister or a young wife would cut off all her beautiful hair and disfigure herself by undergoing hardships. Fathers and brothers blackened their faces, and wore only the shabbiest garments. Such was the spectacle that our people presented when the bright autumn was gone and the cold shadow of winter and misfortune had fallen upon us. "We must suffer," said they—"the Great Mystery is offended."

129

A Winter Camp

When I was about twelve years old we wintered upon the Mouse river, west of Turtle mountain. It was one of the coldest winters I ever knew, and was so regarded by the old men of the tribe. The summer before there had been plenty of buffalo upon that side of the Missouri, and our people had made many packs of dried buffalo meat and cached them in different places, so that they could get them in case of need. There were many black-tailed deer and elk along the river, and grizzlies were to be found in the open country. Apparently there was no danger of starvation, so our people thought to winter there; but it proved to be a hard winter.

There was a great snow-fall, and the cold was intense. The snow was too deep for hunting, and the main body of the buffalo had crossed the Missouri, where it was too far to go after them. But there were some smaller herds of the animals scattered about in our vicinity, therefore there was still fresh meat to be had, but it was not secured without a great deal of difficulty.

No ponies could be used. The men hunted on snow-shoes until after the Moon of Sore Eyes (March), when after a heavy thaw a crust was formed on the snow which would scarcely hold a man. It was then that our people hunted buffalo with dogs—an unusual expedient.

Sleds were made of buffalo ribs and hickory saplings, the runners bound with rawhide with the hair side down. These slipped smoothly over the icy crust. Only small men rode on the sleds. When buffalo were reported by the hunting scouts, everybody had his dog team ready. All went under orders from the police, and approached the herd under cover until they came within charging distance.

The men had their bows and arrows, and a few had guns. The huge animals could not run fast in the deep snow. They all followed a leader, trampling out a narrow path. The dogs with their drivers soon caught up with them on each side, and the hunters brought many of them down.

I remember when the party returned, late in the night. The men came in single file, well loaded, and each dog following his master with an equally heavy load. Both men and animals were white with frost.

We boys had waited impatiently for their arrival. As soon as we spied them coming a buffalo hunting whistle was started, and every urchin in the village added his voice to the weird sound, while the dogs who had been left at home joined with us in the chorus. The men, wearing their buffalo moccasins with the hair inside and robes of the same, came home hungry and exhausted.

It is often supposed that the dog in the Indian camp is a useless member of society, but it is not so in the wild life. We found him one of the most useful of domestic animals, especially in an emergency. . . .

The most exciting event of this year was the attack that the Gros Ventres made upon us just as we moved our camp upon the table land back of the river in the spring. We had plenty of meat then and everybody was happy. The grass was beginning to appear and the ponies to grow fat.

One night there was a war dance. A few of our young men had planned to invade the Gros Ventres country, but it seemed that they too had been thinking of us. Everybody was interested in the proposed war party.

"Uncle, are you going too?" I eagerly asked him.

"No," he replied, with a long sigh. "It is the worst time of year to go on the war-path. We shall have plenty of fighting this summer, as we are going to trench upon their territory in our hunts," he added.

The night was clear and pleasant. The war drum was answered by the howls of coyotes on the opposite side of the Mouse river. I was in the throng, watching the braves who were about to go out in search of glory. "I wish I were old enough; I would surely go with this party," I thought. My friend Tatanka was to go. He was several years older than I, and a hero in my eyes. I watched him as he danced with the rest until nearly midnight. Then I came back to our teepee and rolled myself in my buffalo robe and was soon lost in sleep.

Suddenly I was aroused by loud war cries. "'Woo! woo! hay-ay! hay-ay! U we do! U we do!'" I jumped upon my feet, snatched my bow and arrows and rushed out of the teepee, frantically yelling as I went.

"Stop! stop!" screamed Uncheedah, and caught me by my long hair.

By this time the Gros Ventres had encircled our camp, sending volleys of arrows and bullets into our midst. The women were digging ditches in which to put their children.

My uncle was foremost in the battle. The Sioux bravely withstood the assault, although several of our men had already fallen. Many of the enemy were killed in the field around our teepees. The Sioux at last got their ponies and made a counter charge, led by Oyemakasan (my uncle). They cut the Gros Ventre party in two, and drove them off.

My friend Tatanka was killed. I took one of his eagle feathers, thinking I would wear it the first time that I ever went upon the war-path. I thought I would give anything for the opportunity to go against the Gros Ventres, because they killed my friend. The war songs, the wailing for the dead, the howling of the dogs was intolerable to me. Soon after this we broke up our camp and departed for new scenes.

Wild Harvests

When our people lived in Minnesota, a good part of their natural subsistence was furnished by the wild rice, which grew abundantly in all of that region. Around the shores and all over some of the innumerable lakes of the "Land of Sky-blue Water" was this wild cereal found. Indeed, some of the watery fields in those days might be compared in extent and fruitfulness with the fields of wheat on Minnesota's magnificent farms to-day.

The wild rice harvesters came in groups of fifteen to twenty families to a lake, depending upon the size of the harvest. Some of the Indians hunted buffalo upon the prairie at this season, but there were more who preferred to go to the lakes to gather wild rice, fish, gather berries and hunt the deer. There was an abundance of water-fowls among the grain; and really no season of the year was happier than this.

The camping-ground was usually an attractive spot, with shade and cool breezes off the water. The people, while they pitched their teepees upon the heights, if possible, for the sake of a good outlook, actually lived in their canoes upon the placid waters. The happiest of all, perhaps, were the young maidens, who were all day long in their canoes, in twos or threes, and when tired of gathering the wild cereal, would sit in the boats doing their needle-work.

These maidens learned to imitate the calls of the different water-fowls as a sort of signal to the members of a group. Even the old women and the boys adopted signals, so that while the population of the village was lost to sight in a thick field of wild rice, a meeting could be arranged without calling any one by his or her own name. It was a great convenience for those young men who sought opportunity to meet certain maidens, for there were many canoe paths through the rice.

August is the harvest month. There were many preliminary feasts of fish, ducks and venison, and offerings in honor of the "Water Chief," so that there might not be any drowning accident during the harvest. The preparation consisted of a series of feasts and offerings for many days, while women and men were making birch canoes, for nearly every member of the family must be provided with one for this occasion. The blueberry and huckleberry-picking also preceded the rice-gathering.

There were social events which enlivened the camp of the harvesters; such as maidens' feasts, dances and a canoe regatta or two, in which not only the men were participants, but women and young girls as well.

On the appointed day all the canoes were carried to the shore and placed upon the water with prayer and propitiatory offerings. Each family took possession of the allotted field, and tied all the grain in bundles of convenient size, allowing it to stand for a few days. Then they again entered the lake, assigning two persons to each canoe. One manipulated the paddle, while the foremost one gently drew the heads of each bundle toward him and gave it a few strokes with a light rod. This caused the rice to fall into the bottom of the craft. The field was traversed in this manner back and forth until finished.

This was the pleasantest and easiest part of the harvest toil. The real work was when they prepared the rice for use. First of all, it must be made perfectly dry. They would spread it upon buffalo robes and mats, and sometimes upon layers of coarse swamp grass, and dry it in the sun. If the time was short, they would make a scaffold and spread upon it a certain thickness of the green grass and afterward the rice. Under this a fire was made, taking care that the grass did not catch fire.

When all the rice is gathered and dried, the hulling begins. A round hole is dug about two feet deep and the same in diameter. Then the rice is heated over a fire-place, and emptied into the hole while it is hot. A young man, having washed his feet and put on a new pair of moccasins, treads upon it until all is hulled. The women then pour it upon a robe and begin to shake it so that the chaff will be separated by the wind. Some of the rice is browned before being hulled.

During the hulling time there were prizes offered to the young men who could hull quickest and best. There were sometimes from twenty to fifty youths dancing with their feet in these holes.

Pretty moccasins were brought by shy maidens to the youths of their choice, asking them to hull rice. There were daily entertainments which deserved some such name as "hulling bee"—at any rate, we all enjoyed them hugely. The girls brought with them plenty of good things to eat.

When all the rice was prepared for the table, the matter of storing it had to be determined. Caches were dug by each family in a concealed spot, and carefully lined with dry grass and bark. Here they left their surplus stores for a time of need. Our people were very ingenious in covering up all traces of the hidden food. A common trick was to build a fire on top of the mound. As much of the rice as could be carried conveniently was packed in parfleches, or cases made of rawhide, and brought back with us to our village.

After all, the wild Indians could not be justly termed improvident, when their manner of life is taken into consideration. They let nothing go to waste, and labored incessantly during the summer and fall to lay up provision for the inclement season. Berries of all kinds were industriously gathered, and dried in the sun. Even the wild cherries were pounded up, stones and all, made into small cakes and dried for use in soups and for mixing with the pounded jerked meat and fat to form a much-prized Indian delicacy. . . .

I have referred to the opportunities for courting upon the wild rice fields. Indian courtship is very peculiar in many respects; but when you study their daily life you will see the philosophy of their etiquette of love-making. There was no parlor courtship; the life was largely out-of-doors, which was very favorable to the young men.

In a nomadic life where the female members of the family have entire control of domestic affairs, the work is divided among them all. Very often the bringing of the wood and water devolves upon the young maids, and the spring or the woods become the battle-ground of love's warfare. The nearest water may be some distance from the camp, which is all the better. Sometimes, too, there was no wood to be had; and in that case, one would see the young women scattered all over the prairie, gathering buffalo chips for fuel.

This is the way the red men go about to induce the aboriginal maids to listen to their suit. As soon as the youth has returned from the war-path or the chase, he puts on his porcupine-quill embroidered moccasins and leggings, and folds his best robe about him. He brushes his long, glossy hair with a brush made from the tail of the porcupine, perfumes it with scented grass or leaves, then arranges it in two plaits with an otter skin or some other ornament. If he is a warrior, he adds an eagle feather or two.

If he chooses to ride, he takes his best pony. He jumps upon its bare back, simply throwing a part of his robe under him to serve as a saddle, and holding the end of a lariat tied about the animal's neck. He guides him altogether by the motions of his body. These wily ponies seem to enter into the spirit of the occasion, and very often capture the eyes of the maid by their graceful movements, in perfect obedience to their master.

The general custom is for the young men to pull their robes over their heads, leaving only a slit to look through. Sometimes the same is done by the maiden—especially in public courtship.

He approaches the girl while she is coming from the spring. He takes up his position directly in her path. If she is in a hurry or does not care to stop, she goes around him; but if she is willing to stop and listen she puts down on the ground the vessel of water she is carrying.

Very often at the first meeting the maiden does not know who her lover is. He does not introduce himself immediately, but waits until a second meeting. Sometimes she does not see his face at all; and then she will try to find out who he is and what he looks like before they meet again. If he is not a desirable suitor, she will go with her chaperon and end the affair there.

There are times when maidens go in twos, and then there must be two young men to meet them.

There is some courtship in the night time; either in the early part of the evening, on the outskirts of dances and other public affairs, or after everybody is supposed to be asleep. This is the secret courtship. The youth may pull up the tent pins just back of his sweetheart and speak with her during the night. He must be a smart young man to do that undetected, for the grandmother, her chaperon, is usually "all ears."

Elopements are common. There are many reasons for a girl or a youth to defer their wedding. It may be from personal pride of one or both. The well-born are married publicly, and many things are given away in their honor. The maiden may desire to attend a certain number of maidens' feasts before marrying. The youth may be poor, or he may wish to achieve another honor before surrendering to a woman. . . .

When we lived our natural life, there was much singing of war songs, medicine, hunting and love songs. Sometimes there were few words or none, but everything was understood by the inflection. From this I have often thought that there must be a language of dumb beasts.

The crude musical instrument of the Sioux, the flute, was made to appeal to the susceptible ears of the maidens late into the night. There comes to me now the picture of two young men with their robes over their heads, and only a portion of the hand-made and carved *chotanka*, the flute, protruding from its folds. I can see all the maidens slyly turn their heads to listen. . . .

An Adventurous Journey

It must now be about thirty years since our long journey in search of new hunting-grounds, from the Assiniboine river to the Upper Missouri. The buffalo, formerly so abundant between the two rivers, had begun to shun their usual haunts, on account of the great numbers of Canadian half- breeds in that part of the country. There was also the first influx of English sportsmen, whose wholesale methods of destruction wrought such havoc with the herds. These seemingly intelligent animals correctly prophesied to the natives the approach of the pale-face.

As we had anticipated, we found game very scarce as we traveled slowly across the vast plains. There were only herds of antelope and sometimes flocks of waterfowl, with here and there a lonely bull straggling aimlessly along. At first our party was small, but as we proceeded on our way we fell in with some of the western bands of Sioux and Assiniboines, who are close connections.

Each day the camp was raised and marched from ten to twenty miles. One might wonder how such a cavalcade would look in motion. The only vehicles were the primitive travaux drawn by ponies and large Esquimaux dogs. These are merely a pair of shafts fastened on either side of the animal, and trailing on the ground behind. A large basket suspended between the poles, just above the ground, supplied a place for goods and a safe nest for the babies, or an occasional helpless old woman. Most of our effects were carried by pack ponies; and an Indian packer excels all others in quickness and dexterity.

The train was nearly a mile long, headed by a number of old warriors on foot, who carried the filled pipe, and decided when and where to stop. A very warm day made much trouble for the women who had charge of the moving household. The pack dogs were especially unmanageable. They would become very thirsty and run into the water with their loads. The scolding of the women, the singing of the old men and the yelps of the Indian dudes made our progress a noisy one, and like that of a town in motion rather than an ordinary company of travelers.

This journey of ours was not without its exciting episodes. My uncle had left the main body and gone off to the south with a small party, as he was accustomed to do every summer, to seek revenge of some sort on the whites for all the injuries that they had inflicted upon our family. This time he met with

a company of soldiers between Fort Totten and Fort
Berthold, in North Dakota. Somehow, these seven Indians
surprised the troopers in broad daylight, while eating their
dinner, and captured the whole outfit, including nearly all
their mules and one white horse, with such of their provisions
as they cared to carry back with them. No doubt these soldiers reported at the fort that they had been attacked by a
large party of Indians, and I dare say some promotions
rewarded their tale of a brave defense! However, the facts are
just as I have stated them. My uncle brought home the white
horse, and the fine Spanish mules were taken by the others.
Among the things they brought back with them were several
loaves of raised bread, the first I had ever seen, and a great
curiosity. We called it *aguyape tachangu,* or lung bread, from
its spongy consistency.

Although when a successful war-party returns with so
many trophies, there is usually much dancing and hilarity,
there was almost nothing of the kind on this occasion. The
reason was that the enemy made little resistance; and then
there was our old tradition with regard to the whites that
there is no honor in conquering them, as they fight only
under compulsion. Had there really been a battle, and some
of our men been killed, there would have been some enthusiasm. . . .

In our nomadic life there were a few unwritten laws by
which our people were governed. There was a council, a
police force, and an executive officer, who was not always the
chief, but a member of the tribe appointed to this position
for a given number of days. There were also the wise old men
who were constantly in attendance at the council lodge, and
acted as judges in the rare event of the commission of a
crime.

This simple government of ours was supported by the
issue of little sticks about five inches long. There were a hundred or so of these, and they were distributed every few days
by the police or soldiers, who kept account of them. Whoever

received one of these sticks must return it within five or ten days, with a load of provisions. If one was held beyond the stipulated time the police would call the delinquent warrior to account. In case he did not respond, they could come and destroy his tent or take away his weapons. When all the sticks had been returned, they were reissued to other men; and so the council lodge was supported.

It was the custom that no man who had not distinguished himself upon the war-path could destroy the home of another. This was a necessary qualification for the office of an Indian policeman. These policemen must also oversee the hunt, lest some individuals should be well provided with food while others were in want. No man might hunt independently. The game must be carefully watched by the game scouts, and the discovery of a herd reported at once to the council, after which the time and manner of the hunt were publicly announced.

I well recall how the herald announced the near approach of buffaloes. It was supposed that if the little boys could trip up the old man while going his rounds, the success of the hunt was assured. The oftener he was tripped, the more successful it would be! The signal or call for buffaloes was a peculiar whistle. As soon as the herald appeared, all the boys would give the whistle and follow in crowds after the poor old man. Of course he tried to avoid them, but they were generally too quick for him.

There were two kinds of scouts, for hunting and for war. In one sense every Indian was a scout; but there were some especially appointed to serve for a certain length of time. An Indian might hunt every day, besides the regularly organized hunt; but he was liable to punishment at any time. If he could kill a solitary buffalo or deer without disturbing the herd, it was allowed. He might also hunt small game.

In the movable town under such a government as this, there was apt to be inconvenience and actual suffering, since a great body of people were supported only by the daily hunt.

Hence there was a constant disposition to break up into smaller parties, in order to obtain food more easily and freely. Yet the wise men of the Dakotas would occasionally form large bands of from two to five thousand people, who camped and moved about together for a period of some months. It is apparent that so large a body could not be easily supplied with the necessaries of life; but, on the other hand, our enemies respected such a gathering! Of course the nomadic government would do its utmost to hold together as long as possible. The police did all they could to keep in check those parties who were intent upon stealing away.

There were many times, however, when individual bands and even families were justified in seeking to separate themselves from the rest, in order to gain a better support. It was chiefly by reason of this food question that the Indians never established permanent towns or organized themselves into a more formidable nation. . . .

One day, as we were following along the bank of the Upper Missouri, there appeared to be a great disturbance at the head of the cavalcade—so much so that we thought our people had been attacked by a war-party of the Crows or some of the hostile tribes of that region. In spite of the danger, even the women and children hurried forward to join the men—that is to say, as many as were not upon the hunt. Most of the warriors were out, as usual, and only the large boys and the old men were traveling with the women and their domestic effects and little ones.

As we approached the scene of action, we heard loud shouts and the report of fire-arms; but our party was scattered along for a considerable distance, and all was over before we could reach the spot. It was a great grizzly bear who had been bold enough to oppose, single-handed, the progress of several hundred Indians. The council-men, who usually walked a little in advance of the train, were the first to meet the bear, and he was probably deceived by the sight of this advance body, and thus audaciously defied them.

Among these council-men—all retired chiefs and warriors whose ardent zeal for the display of courage had long been cooled, and whose present duties were those of calm deliberation for their people's welfare—there were two old, distinguished war-chiefs. Each of these men still carried his war-lance, wrapped up in decorated buckskin. As the bear advanced boldly toward them, the two old men promptly threw off their robes—an evidence that there still lurked within their breasts the spirit of chivalry and ready courage. Spear in hand, they both sprang forward to combat with the ferocious animal, taking up their positions about ten feet apart.

As they had expected, the fearful beast, after getting up on his haunches and growling savagely, came forward with widely opened jaws. He fixed his eyes upon the left-hand man, who was ready to meet him with uplifted spear, but with one stroke of his powerful paw the weapon was sent to the ground. At the same moment the right-hand man dealt him a stab that penetrated the grizzly's side.

The bear uttered a groan not unlike that of a man, and seized the spear so violently that its owner was thrown to the ground. As the animal drew the lance from its body, the first man, having recovered his own, stabbed him with it on the other side. Upon this, he turned and knocked the old man down, and again endeavored to extract the spear.

By this time all the dogs and men were at hand. Many arrows and balls were sent into the tough hide of the bear. Yet he would probably have killed both his assailants, had it not been for the active small dogs who were constantly upon his heels and annoying him. A deadly rifle shot at last brought him down.

The old men were badly bruised and torn, but both of them recovered, to bear from that day the high-sounding titles of "Fought-the-Bear" and "Conquered-the-Grizzly."

The Laughing Philosopher

There is scarcely anything so exasperating to me as the idea that the natives of this country have no sense of humor and no faculty for mirth. This phase of their character is well understood by those whose fortune or misfortune it has been to live among them day in and day out at their homes. I don't believe I ever heard a real hearty laugh away from the Indians' fireside. I have often spent an entire evening in laughing with them until I could laugh no more. There are evenings when the recognized wit or story-teller of the village gives a free entertainment which keeps the rest of the community in a convulsive state until he leaves them. However, Indian humor consists as much in the gestures and inflections of the voice as in words, and is really untranslatable.

Matogee (Yellow Bear) was a natural humorous speaker, and a very diffident man at other times. He usually said little, but when he was in the mood he could keep a large company in a roar. This was especially the case whenever he met his brother-in-law, Tamedokah.

It was a custom with us Indians to joke more particularly with our brothers-and sisters-in-law. But no one ever complained, or resented any of these jokes, however personal they might be. That would be an unpardonable breach of etiquette.

"Tamedokah, I heard that you tried to capture a buck by holding on to his tail," said Matogee, laughing. "I believe that feat cannot be performed any more; at least, it never has been since the pale-face brought us the knife, the 'mysterious iron,' and the pulverized coal that makes bullets fly. Since our ancestors hunted with stone knives and hatchets, I say, that has never been done."

The fact was that Tamedokah had stunned a buck that day while hunting, and as he was about to dress him the animal got up and attempted to run, whereupon the Indian launched forth to secure his game. He only succeeded in grasping the tail of the deer, and was pulled about all over the meadows and the adjacent woods until the tail came off in his hands. Matogee thought this too good a joke to be lost.

I sat near the door of the tent, and thoroughly enjoyed the story of the comical accident.

"Yes," Tamedokah quietly replied, "I thought I would do something to beat the story of the man who rode a young elk, and yelled frantically for help, crying like a woman."

"Ugh! that was only a legend," retorted Matogee, for it was he who was the hero of this tale in his younger days. "But this is a fresh feat of today. Chankpayuhah said he could not tell which was the most scared, the buck or you," he continued. "He said the deer's eyes were bulging out of their sockets, while Tamedokah's mouth was constantly enlarging toward his ears, and his hair floated on the wind, shaking among the branches of the trees. That will go down with the traditions of our fathers," he concluded with an air of satisfaction.

"It was a singular mishap," admitted Tamedokah.

The pipe had been filled by Matogee and passed to Tamedokah good-naturedly, still with a broad smile on his face. "It must be acknowledged," he resumed, "that you have the strongest kind of a grip, for no one else could hold on as long as you did, and secure such a trophy besides. That tail will do for an eagle feather holder."

By this time the teepee was packed to overflowing. Loud laughter had been heard issuing from the lodge of Matogee, and everybody suspected that he had something good, so many had come to listen.

"I think we should hear the whole matter," said one of the late comers.

The teepee was brightly lit by the burning embers, and all the men were sitting with their knees up against their chests, held in that position by wrapping their robes tightly around loins and knees. This fixed them something in the fashion of a rocking-chair.

"Well, no one saw him except Chankpayuhah," Matogee remarked.

"Yes, yes, he must tell us about it," exclaimed a chorus of voices.

"This is what I saw," the witness began. "I was tracking a buck and a doe. As I approached a small opening at the creek side 'boom!' came a report of the mysterious iron. I remained in a stooping position, hoping to see a deer cross the opening. In this I was not disappointed, for immediately after the report a fine buck dashed forth with Tamedokah close behind him. The latter was holding on to the deer's tail with both hands and his knife was in his mouth, but it soon dropped out. 'Tamedokah,' I shouted, 'haven't you got hold of the wrong animal?' but as I spoke they disappeared into the woods.

"In a minute they both appeared again, and then it was that I began to laugh. I could not stop. It almost killed me. The deer jumped the longest jumps I ever saw. Tamedokah walked the longest paces and was very swift. His hair was whipping the trees as they went by. Water poured down his face. I stood bent forward because I could not straighten my backbone, and was ready to fall when they again disappeared.

"When they came out for the third time it seemed as if the woods and the meadow were moving too. Tamedokah skipped across the opening as if he were a grasshopper learning to hop. I fell down.

"When I came to he was putting water on my face and head, but when I looked at him I fell again, and did not know anything until the sun had passed the mid-sky."

The company was kept roaring all the way through this account, while Tamedokah himself heartily joined in the mirth.

"Ho, ho, ho!" they said; "he has made his name famous in our annals. This will be told of him henceforth.". . .

First Impressions of Civilization

I was scarcely old enough to know anything definite about the "Big Knives," as we called the white men, when the terrible Minnesota massacre broke up our home and I was carried into exile. I have already told how I was adopted into the family of my father's younger brother, when my father was betrayed and imprisoned. We all supposed that he had shared the fate of those who were executed at Mankato, Minnesota.

Now the savage philosophers looked upon vengeance in the field of battle as a lofty virtue. To avenge the death of a relative or of a dear friend was considered a great deed. My uncle, accordingly, had spared no pains to instill into my young mind the obligation to avenge the death of my father and my older brothers. Already I looked eagerly forward to the day when I should find an opportunity to carry out his teachings. Meanwhile, he himself went upon the war-path and returned with scalps every summer. So it may be imagined how I felt toward the Big Knives!

On the other hand, I had heard marvelous things of this people. In some things we despised them; in others we regarded them as wakan (mysterious), a race whose power bordered upon the supernatural. I learned that they had made a "fireboat." I could not understand how they could unite two elements which cannot exist together. I thought the water would put out the fire, and the fire would consume the boat if it had the shadow of a chance. This was to me a preposterous thing! But when I was told that the Big Knives had created a "fire-boat-walks-on-mountains" (a locomotive) it was too much to believe.

"Why," declared my informant, "those who saw this monster move said that it flew from mountain to mountain when it seemed to be excited. They said also that they believed it carried a thunder-bird, for they frequently heard his usual war-whoop as the creature sped along!"

Several warriors had observed from a distance one of the first trains on the Northern Pacific, and had gained an exaggerated impression of the wonders of the pale-face. They had seen it go over a bridge that spanned a deep ravine and it seemed to them that it jumped from one bank to the other. I confess that the story almost quenched my ardor and bravery.

Two or three young men were talking together about this fearful invention.

"However," said one, "I understand that this fire-boat-walks-on-mountains cannot move except on the track made for it."

Although a boy is not expected to join in the conversation of his elders, I ventured to ask: "Then it cannot chase us into any rough country?"

"No, it cannot do that," was the reply, which I heard with a great deal of relief.

I had seen guns and various other things brought to us by the French Canadians, so that I had already some notion of the supernatural gifts of the white man; but I had never before heard such tales as I listened to that morning. It was said that they had bridged the Missouri and Mississippi rivers, and that they made immense houses of stone and brick, piled on top of one another until they were as high as high hills. My brain was puzzled with these things for many a day. Finally I asked my uncle why the Great Mystery gave such power to the *Washechu* (the rich)—sometimes we called them by this name—and not to us Dakotas.

"For the same reason," he answered, "that he gave to Duta the skill to make fine bows and arrows, and to Wachesne no skill to make anything.". . .

"Certainly they are a heartless nation. They have made some of their people servants—yes, slaves! We have never believed in keeping slaves, but it seems that these *Washechu* do! It is our belief that they painted their servants black a long time ago, to tell them from the rest, and now the slaves have children born to them of the same color!

147

"The greatest object of their lives seems to be to acquire possessions—to be rich. They desire to possess the whole world. For thirty years they were trying to entice us to sell them our land. Finally the outbreak gave them all, and we have been driven away from our beautiful country.

"They are a wonderful people. They have divided the day into hours, like the moons of the year. In fact, they measure everything. Not one of them would let so much as a turnip go from his field unless he received full value for it. I understand that their great men make a feast and invite many, but when the feast is over the guests are required to pay for what they have eaten before leaving the house. I myself saw at White Cliff (the name given to St. Paul, Minnesota) a man who kept a brass drum and a bell to call people to his table; but when he got them in he would make them pay for the food!

"I am also informed," said my uncle, "but this I hardly believe, that their Great Chief (President) compels every man to pay him for the land he lives upon and all his personal goods—even for his own existence—every year!" (This was his idea of taxation.) "I am sure we could not live under such a law.

"When the outbreak occurred, we thought that our opportunity had come, for we had learned that the Big Knives were fighting among themselves, on account of a dispute over their slaves. It was said that the Great Chief had allowed slaves in one part of the country and not in another, so there was jealousy, and they had to fight it out. We don't know how true this was.

"There were some praying-men who came to us some time before the trouble arose. They observed every seventh day as a holy day. On that day they met in a house that they had built for that purpose, to sing, pray, and speak of their Great Mystery. I was never in one of these meetings. I understand that they had a large book from which they read. By all accounts they were very different from all other white men we have known, for these never observed any such day, and we never knew them to pray, neither did they ever tell us of their Great Mystery.

"In war they have leaders and war-chiefs of different grades. The common warriors are driven forward like a herd of antelopes to face the foe. It is on account of this manner of fighting—from compulsion and not from personal bravery—that we count no coup on them. A lone warrior can do much harm to a large army of them in a bad country."

It was this talk with my uncle that gave me my first clear idea of the white man.

I was almost fifteen years old when my uncle presented me with a flint-lock gun. The possession of the "mysterious iron," and the explosive dirt, or "pulverized coal," as it is called, filled me with new thoughts. All the war-songs that I had ever heard from childhood came back to me with their heroes. It seemed as if I were an entirely new being—the boy had become a man!

"I am now old enough," said I to myself, "and I must beg my uncle to take me with him on his next war-path. I shall soon be able to go among the whites whenever I wish, and to avenge the blood of my father and my brothers."

I had already begun to invoke the blessing of the Great Mystery. Scarcely a day passed that I did not offer up some of my game, so that he might not be displeased with me. My people saw very little of me during the day, for in solitude I found the strength I needed. I groped about in the wilderness, and determined to assume my position as a man. My boyish ways were departing, and a sullen dignity and composure was taking their place.

The thought of love did not hinder my ambitions. I had a vague dream of some day courting a pretty maiden, after I had made my reputation, and won the eagle feathers.

One day, when I was away on the daily hunt, two strangers from the United States visited our camp. They had boldly ventured across the northern border. They were Indians, but clad in the white man's garments. It was as well that I was absent with my gun.

My father, accompanied by an Indian guide, after many days' searching had found us at last. He had been imprisoned at Davenport, Iowa, with those who took part in the massacre or in the battles following, and he was taught in prison and converted by the pioneer missionaries, Drs. Williamson and Riggs. He was under sentence of death, but was among the number against whom no direct evidence was found, and who were finally pardoned by President Lincoln.

When he was released, and returned to the new reservation upon the Missouri river, he soon became convinced that life on a government reservation meant physical and moral degradation. Therefore he determined, with several others, to try the white man's way of gaining a livelihood. They accordingly left the agency against the persuasions of the agent, renounced all government assistance, and took land under the United States Homestead law, on the Big Sioux river. After he had made his home there, he desired to seek his lost child. It was then a dangerous undertaking to cross the line, but his Christian love prompted him to do it. He secured a good guide, and found his way in time through the vast wilderness.

As for me, I little dreamed of anything unusual to happen on my return. As I approached our camp with my game on my shoulder, I had not the slightest premonition that I was suddenly to be hurled from my savage life into a life unknown to me hitherto.

When I appeared in sight my father, who had patiently listened to my uncle's long account of my early life and training, became very much excited. He was eager to embrace the child who, as he had just been informed, made it already the object of his life to avenge his father's blood. The loving father could not remain in the teepee and watch the boy coming, so he started to meet him. My uncle arose to go with his brother to insure his safety.

My face burned with the unusual excitement caused by the sight of a man wearing the Big Knives' clothing and coming toward me with my uncle.

"What does this mean, uncle?"

"My boy, this is your father, my brother, whom we mourned as dead. He has come for you."

My father added: "I am glad that my son is strong and brave. Your brothers have adopted the white man's way; I came for you to learn this new way, too; and I want you to grow up a good man."

He had brought me some civilized clothing, At first, I disliked very much to wear garments made by the people I had hated so bitterly. But the thought that, after all, they had not killed my father and brothers, reconciled me, and I put on the clothes.

In a few days we started for the States. I felt as if I were dead and traveling to the Spirit Land; for now all my old ideas were to give place to new ones, and my life was to be entirely different from that of the past.

Still, I was eager to see some of the wonderful inventions of the white people. When we reached Fort Totten, I gazed about me with lively interest and a quick imagination.

My father had forgotten to tell me that the fire-boat-walks-on-mountains had its track at Jamestown, and might appear at any moment. As I was watering the ponies, a peculiar shrilling noise pealed forth from just beyond the hills. The ponies threw back their heads and listened; then they ran snorting over the prairie. Meanwhile, I too had taken alarm. I leaped on the back of one of the ponies, and dashed off at full speed. It was a clear day; I could not imagine what had caused such an unearthly noise. It seemed as if the world were about to burst in two!

I got upon a hill as the train appeared. "O!" I said to myself, "that is the fire-boat-walks-on-mountains that I have heard about!" Then I drove back the ponies.

My father was accustomed every morning to read from his Bible, and sing a stanza of a hymn. I was about very early with my gun for several mornings; but at last he stopped me as I was preparing to go out, and bade me wait.

I listened with much astonishment. The hymn contained the word Jesus. I did not comprehend what this meant; and my father then told me that Jesus was the Son of God who came on earth to save sinners, and that it was because of him that he had sought me. This conversation made a deep impression upon my mind.

Late in the fall we reached the citizen settlement at Flandreau, South Dakota, where my father and some others dwelt among the whites. Here my wild life came to an end, and my school days began.

Selections from

From the Deep Woods to Civilization
1916

The Way Opens

One can never be sure of what a day may bring to pass. At
the age of fifteen years, the deepening current of my life
swung upon such a pivotal day, and in the twinkling of an eye
its whole course was utterly changed; as if a little mountain
brook should pause and turn upon itself to gather strength
for the long journey toward an unknown ocean.

From childhood I was consciously trained to be a man;
that was, after all, the basic thing; but after this I was trained
to be a warrior and a hunter, and not to care for money or
possessions, but to be in the broadest sense a public servant.
After arriving at a reverent sense of the pervading presence
of the Spirit and Giver of Life, and a deep consciousness of
the brotherhood of man, the first thing for me to accomplish
was to adapt myself perfectly to natural things—in other
words, to harmonize myself with nature. To this end I was
made to build a body both symmetrical and enduring—a
house for the soul to live in—a sturdy house, defying the elements. I must have faith and patience; I must learn self-control and be able to maintain silence. I must do with as little as
possible and start with nothing most of the time, because a
true Indian always shares whatever he may possess.

I felt no hatred for our tribal foes. I looked upon them
more as the college athlete regards his rivals from another
college. There was no thought of destroying a nation, taking
away their country or reducing the people to servitude, for
my race rather honored and bestowed gifts upon their enemies at the next peaceful meeting, until they had adopted the

usages of the white man's warfare for spoliation and conquest.

There was one unfortunate thing about my early training, however; that is, I was taught never to spare a citizen of the United States, although we were on friendly terms with the Canadian white men. The explanation is simple. My people had been turned out of some of the finest country in the world, now forming the great states of Minnesota and Iowa. The Americans pretended to buy the land at ten cents an acre, but never paid the price; the debt stands unpaid to this day. Because they did not pay, the Sioux protested; finally came the outbreak of 1862 in Minnesota, when many settlers were killed, and forthwith our people, such as were left alive, were driven by the troops into exile.

My father, who was among the fugitives in Canada, had been betrayed by a half-breed across the United States line, near what is now the city of Winnipeg. Some of the party were hanged at Fort Snelling, near St. Paul. We supposed, and, in fact, we were informed that all were hanged. This was why my uncle, in whose family I lived, had taught me never to spare a white man from the United States.

During the summer and winter of 1871, the band of Sioux to which I belonged—a clan of the *Wahpetons,* or "Dwellers among the Leaves"—roamed in the upper Missouri region and along the Yellowstone River. In that year I tasted to the full the joy and plenty of wild existence. I saw buffalo, elk, and antelope in herds numbering thousands. The forests teemed with deer, and in the "Bad Lands" dwelt the Big Horns or Rocky Mountain sheep. At this period, grizzly bears were numerous and were brought into camp quite commonly, like any other game.

We frequently met and camped with the Hudson Bay half-breeds in their summer hunt of the buffalo, and we were on terms of friendship with the Assiniboines and the Crees, but in frequent collision with the Blackfeet, the Gros Ventres, and the Crows. However, there were times of truce when all met in peace for a great midsummer festival and exchange of gifts. The Sioux roamed over an area nearly a thousand miles in extent. In the summer we gathered together in large numbers, but towards fall we would divide into small groups or bands and scatter for the trapping and the winter hunt. Most of us hugged the wooded river bottoms; some depended entirely upon the buffalo for food, while others, and among these my immediate kindred, hunted all kinds of game, and trapped and fished as well.

Thus I was trained thoroughly for an all-round out-door life and for all natural emergencies. I was a good rider and a good shot with the bow and arrow, alert and alive to everything that came within my ken. I had never known nor ever expected to know any life but this.

In the winter and summer of 1872, we drifted toward the southern part of what is now Manitoba. In this wild, rolling country I rapidly matured, and laid, as I supposed, the foundations of my life career, never dreaming of anything beyond this manful and honest, unhampered existence. My horse and my dog were my closest companions. I regarded them as brothers, and if there was a hereafter, I expected to meet them there. With them I went out daily into the wilderness to seek inspiration and store up strength for coming manhood. My teachers dreamed no more than I of any change in my prospects. I had now taken part in all our tribal activities except that of war, and was nearly old enough to be initiated into the ritual of the war-path. The world was full of natural rivalry; I was eager for the day.

I had attained the age of fifteen years and was about to enter into and realize a man's life, as we Indians understood it, when the change came. One fine September morning as I returned from the daily hunt, there seemed to he an unusual stir and excitement as I approached our camp. My faithful grandmother was on the watch and met me to break the news. "Your father has come—he whom we thought dead at the hands of the white men," she said.

It was a day of miracle in the deep Canadian wilderness, before the Canadian Pacific had been even dreamed of, while the Indian and the buffalo still held sway over the vast plains of Manitoba east of the Rocky Mountains. It was, perhaps, because he was my honored father that I lent my bewildered ear to his eloquent exposition of the so-called civilized life, or the way of the white man. I could not doubt my own father, so mysteriously come back to us, as it were, from the spirit land; yet there was a voice within saying to me, "A false life! a treacherous life!"

In accordance with my training, I asked few questions, although many arose in my mind. I simply tried silently to fit the new ideas like so many blocks into the pattern of my philosophy, while according to my un-tutored logic some did not seem to have straight sides or square corners to fit in with the cardinal principles of eternal justice. My father had been converted by Protestant missionaries, and he gave me a totally new vision of the white man, as a religious man and a kindly. But when he related how he had set apart every seventh day for religious duties and the worship of God, laying aside every other occupation on that day, I could not forbear exclaiming, "Father! and does he then forget God during the six days and do as he pleases?"

"Our own life, I will admit, is the best in a world of our own, such as we have enjoyed for ages," said my father. "But here is a race which has learned to weigh and measure everything, time and labor and the results of labor, and has learned to accumulate and preserve both wealth and the records of experience for future generations. You yourselves know and use some of the wonderful inventions of the white man, such as guns and gunpowder, knives and hatchets, garments of every description, and there are thousands of other things both beautiful and useful.

"Above all, they have their Great Teacher, whom they call Jesus, and he taught them to pass on their wisdom and knowledge to all other races. It is true that they have subdued and taught many peoples, and our own must eventually bow to this law; the sooner we accept their mode of life and follow their teaching, the better it will be for us all. I have thought much on this matter and such is my conclusion."

There was a mingling of admiration and indignation in my mind as I listened. My father's two brothers were still far from being convinced; but filial duty and affection over-weighed all my prejudices. I was bound to go back with him as he desired me to do, and my grandmother and her only daughter accompanied us on the perilous journey.

The line between Canada and the United States was close-ly watched at this time by hostile Indians, therefore my father thought it best to make a dash for Devil's Lake, in North Dakota, where he could get assistance if necessary. . . .

One of the first things I observed was my father's reading aloud from a book every morning and evening, followed by a very strange song and a prayer. Although all he said was in Indian, I did not understand it fully. He apparently talked aloud to the "Great Mystery", asking for our safe guidance back to his home in the States. The first reading of this book of which I have any recollection was the twenty-third Psalm, and the first hymn he sang in my presence was to the old tune of Ortonville. It was his Christian faith and devotion which was perhaps the strongest influence toward my change of heart and complete change of my purpose in life. . . .

After a variety of adventures, we arrived at the canvas city of Jamestown, then the terminal point of the Northern Pacific railroad. I was out watering the ponies when a terrific peal of thunder burst from a spotless blue sky, and indeed seemed to me to be running along the surface of the ground. The terrified ponies instantly stampeded, and I confess I was not far behind them, when a monster with one fiery eye poked his head around a corner of the hill. When we reached camp, my father kindly explained, and I was greatly relieved.

It was a peaceful Indian summer day when we reached Flandreau, in Dakota Territory, the citizen Indian settlement, and found the whole community gathered together to congratulate and welcome us home.

My First School Days

It was less than a month since I had been a rover and a hunter in the Manitoba wilderness, with no thoughts save those which concern the most free and natural life of an Indian. Now, I found myself standing near a rude log cabin on the edge of a narrow strip of timber, overlooking the fertile basin of the Big Sioux River. As I gazed over the rolling prairie land, all I could see was that it met the sky at the horizon line. It seemed to me vast and vague and endless, as was my conception of the new trail which I had taken and my dream of the far-off goal.

My father's farm of 160 acres, which he had taken up and improved under the United States homestead laws, lay along the north bank of the river. The nearest neighbor lived a mile away, and all had flourishing fields of wheat, Indian corn and potatoes. Some two miles distant, where the Big Sioux doubled upon itself in a swinging loop, rose the mission church and schoolhouse, the only frame building within forty miles.

Our herd of ponies was loose upon the prairie, and it was my first task each morning to bring them into the log corral. On this particular morning I lingered, finding some of them, like myself, who loved their freedom too well and would not come in.

The man who had built the cabin—it was his first house, and therefore he was proud of it—was tall and manly looking. He stood in front of his pioneer home with a resolute face.

He had been accustomed to the buffalo-skin teepee all his life, until he opposed the white man and was defeated and made a prisoner of war at Davenport, Iowa. It was because of his meditations during those four years in a military prison that he had severed himself from his tribe and taken up a homestead. He declared that he would never join in another

Indian outbreak, but would work with his hands for the rest of his life.

"I have hunted every day," he said, "for the support of my family. I sometimes chase the deer all day. One must work, and work hard, whether chasing the deer or planting corn. After all, the corn-planting is the surer provision."

These were my father's new views, and in this radical change of life he had persuaded a few other families to join him. They formed a little colony at Flandreau, on the Big Sioux River.

To be sure, his beginnings in civilization had not been attended with all the success that he had hoped for. One year the crops had been devoured by grasshoppers, and another year ruined by drought. But he was still satisfied that there was no alternative for the Indian. He was now anxious to have his boys learn the English language and something about books, for he could see that these were the "bow and arrows" of the white man.

"O-hee-ye-sa! called my father, and I obeyed the call. "It is time for you to go to school, my son," he said, with his usual air of decision. We had spoken of the matter more than once, yet it seemed hard when it came to the actual undertaking.

I remember quite well how I felt as I stood there with eyes fixed upon the ground.

"And what am I to do at the school?" I asked finally, with much embarrassment.

"You will be taught the language of the white man, and also how to count your money and tell the prices of your horses and of your furs. The white teacher will first teach you the signs by which you can make out the words on their books. They call them A, B, C, and so forth. Old as I am, I have learned some of them."

The matter having been thus far explained, I was soon on my way to the little mission school, two miles distant over the prairie. There was no clear idea in my mind as to what I had to do, but as I galloped along the road I turned over and over what my father had said, and the more I thought of it the less I was satisfied. Finally I said aloud:

"Why do we need a sign language, when we can both hear and talk?" And unconsciously I pulled on the lariat and the pony came to a stop. I suppose I was half curious and half in dread about this "learning white men's ways." Meanwhile the pony had begun to graze.

While thus absorbed in thought, I was suddenly startled by the yells of two other Indian boys and the noise of their ponies' hoofs. I pulled the pony's head up just as the two strangers also pulled up and stopped their panting ponies at my side. They stared at me for a minute, while I looked at them out of the corners of my eyes.

"Where are you going? Are you going to our school?" volunteered one of the boys at last.

To this I replied timidly: "My father told me to go to a place where the white men's ways are taught, and to learn the sign language."

"That's good we are going there too! Come on, Red Feather, let's try another race! I think, if we had not stopped, my pony would have outrun yours. Will you race with us?" he continued, addressing me; and we all started our ponies at full speed.

I soon saw that the two strange boys were riding erect and soldier-like. "That must be because they have been taught to be like the white man," I thought. I allowed my pony a free start and leaned forward until the animal drew deep breaths, then I slid back and laid my head against the pony's shoulder, at the same time raising my quirt, and he leaped forward with a will! I yelled as I passed the other boys, and pulled up when I reached the crossing. The others stopped, too, and surveyed pony and rider from head to foot, as if they had never seen us before.

"You have a fast pony. Did you bring him back with you from Canada?" Red Feather asked. "I think you are the son of

Many Lightnings, whom he brought home the other day," the boy added.

"Yes, this is my own pony. My uncle in Canada always used him to chase the buffalo, and he has ridden him in many battles." I spoke with considerable pride.

"Well, as there are no more buffalo to chase now, your pony will have to pull the plow like the rest. But if you ride him to school, you can join in the races. On the holy days the young men race horses, too."

Red Feather and White Fish spoke both together, while I listened attentively, for everything was strange to me.

"What do you mean by the 'holy days'?" I asked.

"Well, that's another of the white people's customs. Every seventh day they call a 'holy day', and on that day they go to a 'Holy House', where they pray to their Great Mystery. They also say that no one should work on that day."

This definition of Sunday and churchgoing set me to thinking again, for I never knew before that there was any difference in the days.

"But how do you count the days, and how do you know what day to begin with?" I inquired.

"Oh, that's easy! The white men have everything in their books. They know how many days in a year, and they have even divided the day itself into so many equal parts; in fact, they have divided them again and again until they know how many times one can breathe in a day," said White Fish, with the air of a learned man.

"That's impossible," I thought, so I shook my head.

By this time we had reached the second crossing of the river, on whose bank stood the little mission school. Thirty or forty Indian children stood about, curiously watching the newcomer as we came up the steep bank. I realized for the first time that I was an object of curiosity, and it was not a pleasant feeling. On the other hand, I was considerably interested in the strange appearance of these school-children.

They all had on some apology for white man's clothing, but their pantaloons belonged neither to the order *short* nor to the *long*. Their coats, some of them, met only halfway by the help of long strings. Others were lapped over in front, and held on by a string of some sort fastened round the body. Some of their hats were brimless and others without crowns, while most were fantastically painted. The hair of all the boys was cut short, and, in spite of the evidences of great effort to keep it down, it stood erect like porcupine quills. I thought, as I stood on one side and took a careful observation of the motley gathering, that if I had to look like these boys in order to obtain something of the white man's learning, it was time for me to rebel.

The boys played ball and various other games, but I tied my pony to a tree and then walked up to the schoolhouse and stood there as still as if I had been glued to the wall. Presently the teacher came out and rang a bell, and all the children went in, but I waited for some time before entering, and then slid inside and took the seat nearest the door. I felt singularly out of place, and for the twentieth time wished my father had not sent me.

When the teacher spoke to me, I had not the slightest idea what he meant, so I did not trouble myself to make any demonstration, for fear of giving offense. Finally he asked in broken Sioux: "What is your name?" Evidently he had not been among the Indians long, or he would not have asked that question. It takes a tactician and a diplomat to get an Indian to tell his name! The poor man was compelled to give up the attempt and resume his seat on the platform.

He then gave some unintelligible directions, and, to my great surprise, the pupils in turn held their books open and talked the talk of a strange people. Afterward the teacher made some curious signs upon a blackboard on the wall, and seemed to ask the children to read them. To me they did not compare in interest with my bird's-track and fish-fin studies on the sands. I was something like a wild cub caught overnight, and appearing in the corral next morning with the lambs. I had seen nothing thus far to prove to me the good of civilization.

Meanwhile the children grew more familiar, and whispered references were made to the "new boy's" personal appearance. At last he was called "Baby" by one of the big boys; but this was not meant for him to hear, so he did not care to hear. He rose silently and walked out. He did not dare to do or say anything in departing. The boys watched him as he led his pony to the river to drink and then jumped upon his back and started for home at a good pace. They cheered as he started over the hills: "Hoo-oo! hoo-oo! there goes the long-haired boy!"

When I was well out of sight of the school, I pulled in my pony and made him walk slowly home.

"Will going to that place make a man brave and strong?" I asked myself. "I must tell my father that I cannot stay here. I must go back to my uncle in Canada, who taught me to hunt and shoot and to be a brave man. They might as well try to make a buffalo build houses like a beaver as to teach me to be a white man," I thought. It was growing late when at last I appeared at the cabin. "Why, what is the matter?" quoth my old grandmother, who had taken especial pride in me as a promising young hunter. Really, my face had assumed a look of distress and mental pressure that frightened the superstitious old woman. She held her peace, however, until my father returned.

"Ah," she said then, "I never fully believed in these new manners! The Great Mystery cannot make a mistake. I say it is against our religion to change the customs that have been practiced by our people ages back—so far back that no one can remember it. Many of the school-children have died, you have told me. It is not strange. You have offended Him, because you have made these children change the ways he has given us. I must know more about this matter before I give my consent." Grandmother had opened her mind in unmistakable terms, and the whole family was listening to her in silence.

Then my hard-headed father broke the pause. "Here is one Sioux who will sacrifice everything to win the wisdom of the white man! We have now entered upon this life, and there is no going back. Besides, one would be like a hobbled pony without learning to live like those among whom we must live."

During father's speech my eyes had been fixed upon the burning logs that stood on end in the huge mud chimney in a corner of the cabin. I didn't want to go to that place again; but father's logic was too strong for me, and the next morning I had my long hair cut, and started in to school in earnest.

I obeyed my father's wishes, and went regularly to the little day-school, but as yet my mind was in darkness. What has all this talk of books to do with hunting, or even with planting corn? I thought. The subject occupied my thoughts more and more, doubtless owing to my father's decided position on the matter; while, on the other hand, my grandmother's view of this new life was not encouraging.

I took the situation seriously enough, and I remember I went with it where all my people go when they want light— into the thick woods. I needed counsel, and human counsel did not satisfy me. I had been taught to seek the "Great Mystery" in silence, in the deep forest or on the height of the mountain. There were no mountains here, so I retired into the woods. I knew nothing of the white man's religion; I only followed the teaching of my ancestors.

When I came back, my heart was strong. I desired to follow the new trail to the end. I knew that, like the little brook, it must lead to larger and larger ones until it became a resistless river, and I shivered to think of it. But again I recalled the teachings of my people, and determined to imitate their undaunted bravery and stoic resignation.

However, I was far from having realized the long, tedious years of study and confinement before I could begin to achieve what I had planned.

"You must not fear to work with your hands," said my father, "but if you are able to think strongly and well, that will be a quiver full of arrows for you, my son. All of the white man's children must go to school, but those who study best and longest need not work with their hands after that, for they can work with their minds. You may plow the five acres next the river, and see if you can make a straight furrow as well as a straight shot.". . .

It appears remarkable to me now that my father, thorough Indian as he was, should have had such deep and sound conceptions of a true civilization. But there is the contrast— my father's mother, whose faith in her people's philosophy and training could not be superseded by any other allegiance.

To her such a life as we lead today would be no less than sacrilege. "It is not a true life," she often said. "It is a sham. I cannot bear to see my boy live a made-up life!"

Grandmother! you have forgotten one of the first principles of your own teaching, namely: "When you see a new trail, or a footprint that you do not know, follow it to the point of knowing."

"All I want to say to you," the old grandmother seems to answer, "is this: Do not get lost on this new trail."

"I find," said my father to me, "that the white man has a well-grounded religion, and teaches his children the same virtues that our people taught to theirs. The Great Mystery has shown to the red and white man alike the good and evil, from which to choose. I think the way of the white man is better than ours, because he is able to preserve on paper the things he does not want to forget. He records everything— the sayings of his wise men, the laws enacted by his counselors."

I began to be really interested in this curious scheme of living that my father was gradually unfolding to me out of his limited experience.

"The way of knowledge," he continued, "is like our old way in hunting. You begin with a mere trail—a footprint. If you follow that faithfully, it may lead you to a clearer trail—a track—a road. Later on there will be many tracks, crossing and diverging one from the other. Then you must be careful, for success lies in the choice of the right road. You must be doubly careful, for traps will be laid for you, of which the most dangerous is the spirit-water, that causes a man to forget his self-respect," he added, unwittingly giving to his aged mother material for her argument against civilization.

The general effect upon me of these discussions, which were logical enough on the whole, although almost entirely from the outside, was that I became convinced that my father was right.

My grandmother had to yield at last, and it was settled that I was to go to school at Santee agency, Nebraska, where Dr. Alfred L. Riggs was then fairly started in the work of his great mission school, which has turned out some of the best educated Sioux Indians. It was at that time the Mecca of the Sioux country; even though Sitting Bull and Crazy Horse were still at large, harassing soldiers and emigrants alike, and General Custer had just been placed in military command of the Dakota Territory.

On the White Man's Trail

It was in the fall of 1874 that I started from Flandreau, then only an Indian settlement, . . . There were only a dozen houses or so at Sioux Falls, and the whole country was practically uninhabited, when we embarked in a home-made prairie schooner, on that bright September morning.

I had still my Hudson Bay flintlock gun, which I had brought down with me from Canada the year before. I took that old companion, with my shot-pouch and a well-filled powder-horn. All I had besides was a blanket, and an extra shirt. I wore my hunting suit, which was a compromise between Indian attire and a frontiersman's outfit. I was about sixteen years old and small for my age.

"Remember, my boy, it is the same as if I sent you on your first war-path. I shall expect you to conquer," was my father's farewell. My good grandmother, who had brought me up as a motherless child, bestowed upon me her blessing. "Always remember," said she, "that the Great Mystery is good; evil can come only from ourselves!" Thus I parted with my first teacher—the woman who taught me to pray! . . .

"Tell my father," I said, "that I shall not return until I finish my war-path."

But the voice of the waterfall, near what is now the city of Sioux Falls, sounded like the spirits of woods and water crying for their lost playmate, and I thought for a moment of turning back to Canada, there to regain my freedom and wild life. Still, I had sent word to my father that this warpath should be completed, and I remembered how he had said that if I did not return, he would shed proud tears.

About this time I did some of the hardest thinking that I have ever done in my life. . . .

When I reached the back hills of the Missouri, there lay before me a long slope leading to the river bottom, and upon the broad flat, as far as my eyes could reach, lay farm-houses and farms. Ah! I thought, this is the way of civilization, the basis upon which it rests! I desired to know that life.

. . . A little further on I met the Indian agent, Major Sears, a Quaker, and he, too, gave me a word of encouragement when he learned that I had walked a hundred and fifty miles to school. My older brother John, who was then assistant teacher and studying under Dr. Riggs, met me at the school and introduced me to my new life.

The bell of the old chapel at Santee summoned the pupils to class. Our principal read aloud from a large book and offered prayer. Although he conducted devotional exercises in the Sioux language, the subject matter was still strange, and the names he used were unintelligible to me. "Jesus" and "Jehovah" fell upon my ears as mere meaningless sounds.

I understood that he was praying to the "Great Mystery" that the work of the day might be blessed and their labor be fruitful. A cold sweat came out upon me as I heard him ask the "Great Mystery" to be with us in that day's work in that school building. I thought it was too much to ask of Him. I had been taught that the Supreme Being is only concerned with spirits, and that when one wishes to commune with Him in nature he must be in a spiritual attitude, and must retire from human sound or influence, alone in the wilderness. Here for the first time I heard Him addressed openly in the presence of a house full of young men and young girls! . . .

Next morning the day pupils emerged in every direction from the woods and deep ravines where the Indians had made their temporary homes, while we, the log-cabin boarders, came out in Indian file. The chapel bell was tolling as we reached the yard, when my attention was attracted to a pretty lass standing with her parents and Dr. Riggs near the Dakota Home. Then they separated and the father and mother came toward us, leaving the Doctor and the pretty Dakota maiden standing still. All at once the girl began to run toward her parents, screaming pitifully.

"Oh, I cannot, I cannot stay in the white man's house! I'll die, I'll die! Mamma! Mamma!"

The parents stopped and reasoned with the girl, but it was of no use. Then I saw. them leading her back to the Dakota Home, in spite of her pleading and begging. The scene made my blood boil, and I suppressed with difficulty a strong desire to go to her aid.

How well I remember the first time we were called upon to recite! In the same primer class were Eagle-Crane, Kite, and their compatriot from up the river. For a whole week we youthful warriors were held up and harassed with words of three letters. Like raspberry bushes in the path, they tore, bled, and sweated us—those little words rat, cat, and so forth—until not a semblance of our native dignity and self-respect was left. And we were of just the age when the Indian youth is most on his dignity! Imagine the same fellows turned loose against Custer or Harney with anything like equal numbers and weapons, and those tried generals would feel like boys! We had been bred and trained to those things; but when we found ourselves within four walls and set to pick out words of three letters we were like novices upon snow-shoes—often flat on the ground.

I hardly think I was ever tired in my life until those first days of boarding-school. All day things seemed to come and pass with a wearisome regularity, like walking railway ties—the step was too short for me. At times I felt something of the fascination of the new life, and again there would arise in me a dogged resistance, and a voice seemed to be saying, "It is cowardly to depart from the old things!"

Aside from repeating and spelling words, we had to count and add imaginary amounts. We never had had any money to count, nor potatoes, nor turnips, nor bricks. Why, we valued nothing except honor; that cannot be purchased! It seemed now that everything must be measured in time or money or distance. And when the teacher placed before us a painted globe, and said that our world was like that—that upon such a thing our forefathers had roamed and hunted for untold ages, as it whirled and danced around the sun in space—I felt that my foothold was deserting me. All my savage training and philosophy was in the air, if these things were true.

Later on, when Dr. Riggs explained to us the industries of the white man, his thrift and forethought, we could see the reasonableness of it all. Economy is the able assistant of labor, and the two together produce great results. The systems and methods of business were of great interest to us, and especially the adoption of a medium of exchange.

The Doctor's own personality impressed us deeply, and his words of counsel and daily prayers, strange to us at first, in time found root in our minds. Next to my own father, this man did more than perhaps any other to make it possible for me to grasp the principles of true civilization. He also strengthened and developed in me that native strong ambition to win out, by sticking to whatever I might undertake. . . .

My father wrote to me in the Dakota language for my encouragement. Dr. Riggs had told him that I was not afraid of books or of work, but rather determined to profit by them. "My son," he wrote, "I believe that an Indian can learn all that is in the books of the white man, so that he may be equal to them in the ways of the mind!"

I studied harder than most of the boys. Missionaries were poor, and the Government policy of education for the Indian had not then been developed. The white man in general had no use for the Indian. Sitting Bull and the Northern Cheyennes were still fighting in Wyoming and Montana, so that the outlook was not bright for me to pursue my studies among the whites, yet it was now my secret dream and ambition. . . .

Although I could not understand or speak much English, at the end of my second year I could translate every word of my English studies into the native tongue, besides having read all that was then published in the Sioux. I had caught up with boys who had two or three years the start of me, and was now studying elementary algebra and geometry.

One day Dr. Riggs came to me and said that he had a way by which he could send me to Beloit, Wisconsin, to enter the preparatory department of Beloit College. This was a great opportunity, and I grasped it eagerly, though I had not yet lost my old timidity about venturing alone among the white people.

On the eve of departure, I received word from Flandreau that my father was dead, after only two days' illness. He was still in the prime of life and a tireless worker. This was a severe shock to me, but I felt even more strongly that I must carry out his wishes. It was clear that he who had sought me out among the wild tribes at the risk of his life, and set my feet in the new trail, should be obeyed to the end. I did not go back to my home, but in September, 1876, I started from Santee to Beloit to begin my serious studies.

College Life in the West

The journey to Beloit College was an education in itself. At Yankton City I boarded the train for the first time in my life, but not before having made a careful inspection of the locomotive—that fiery monster which had so startled me on my way home from Canada. Every hour brought new discoveries and new thoughts—visions that came and passed like the telegraph poles as we sped by. More and more we seemed to me to be moving upon regions too small for the inhabitants. Towns and villages grew ever larger and nearer together, until at last we reached a city of some little size where it was necessary for me to change cars, a matter that had been arranged by Dr. Riggs with the conductor. The streets looked crowded and everybody seemed to be in the greatest possible hurry. I was struck with the splendor of the shops and the brilliant show windows. Someone took me to an eating house and left me alone with the pretty waitress, whose bright eyes and fluent speech alarmed me. I thought it best to agree with everything she said, so I assented with a nod of the head, and I fancy she brought me everything that was on the bill of fare!

When I reached Beloit on the second day of my pilgrimage, I found it beautifully located on the high, wooded banks of Black Hawk's picturesque Rock River. The college grounds covered the site of an ancient village of mound-builders, which showed to great advantage on the neat campus, where the green grass was evenly cut with lawn . . .

It must be remembered that this was September, 1876, less than three months after Custer's gallant command was annihilated by the hostile Sioux. I was especially troubled when I learned that my two uncles whom we left in Canada had taken part in this famous fight. People were bitter against the Sioux in those days, and I think it was a local paper that printed the story that I was a nephew of Sitting Bull, who had sent me there to study the white man's arts so that he might be better able to cope with him. When I went into the town, I was followed on the streets by gangs of little white savages, giving imitation war whoops.

. . . I made every effort and soon learned to speak quite fluently, although not correctly; but that fact did not discourage me.

I was now a stranger in a strange country, and deep in a strange life from which I could not retreat. I was like a deaf man with eyes continually on the alert for the expression of faces, and to find them in general friendly toward me was somewhat reassuring. In spite of some nerve-trying moments, I soon recovered my balance and set to work. I absorbed knowledge through every pore. The more I got, the larger my capacity grew, and my appetite increased in proportion. I discovered that my anticipations of this new life were nearly all wrong, and was suddenly confronted with problems entirely foreign to my experience. If I had been told to swim across a lake, or run with a message through an unknown country, I should have had some conception of the task; but the idea of each word as having an office and a place and a specific name, and standing in relation to other words like the bricks in a wall, was almost beyond my grasp. As for history and geography, to me they were legends and traditions, and I soon learned to appreciate the pure logic of mathematics. . . .

At Beloit I spent three years of student life. While in some kinds of knowledge I was the infant of the college, in athletics I did my full share. To keep myself at my best physically, I spent no less than three hours daily in physical exercise, and this habit was kept up throughout my college days.

I found among the students many who were self-support-
ing, either the sons of poor parents, or self-reliant youth who
preferred to earn money for at least a part of their expenses.
I soon discovered that these young men were usually among
the best students. Since I had no means of my own, and the
United States Government had not then formulated the policy of Indian education, I was ready for any kind of work, and
on Saturdays I usually sawed wood and did other chores for
the professors. . . .

It was here and now that my eyes were opened intelli-
gently to the greatness of Christian civilization, the ideal civilization, as it unfolded itself before my eyes. I saw it as the
development of every natural resource; the broad brotherhood of mankind; the blending of all languages and the gathering of all races under one religious faith. There must be no
more warfare within our borders; we must quit the forest trail
for the breaking-plow, since pastoral life was the next thing
for the Indian. I renounced finally my bow and arrows for the
spade and the pen; I took off my soft moccasins and put on
the heavy and clumsy but durable shoes. Every day of my life
I put into use every English word that I knew, and for the first
time permitted myself to think and act as a white man.

At the end of three years, . . . Dr. Riggs arranged to transfer me to the preparatory department of Knox College, at
Galesburg, Ill., of which he was himself a graduate. Here,
again, I was thrown into close contact with the rugged, ambitious sons of western farmers. . . .

As Knox is a co-educational institution, it was here that I
mingled for the first time with the pale-face maidens, and as
soon as I could shake off my Indian shyness, I found them
very winning and companionable. It was through social intercourse with the American college girl that I gained my first
conception of the home life and domestic ideals of the white
man. . . .

Soon I began to lay definite plans for the future. Happily,
I had missed the demoralizing influences of reservation life,

and had been mainly thrown with the best class of Christian white people. With all the strength of a clean young manhood, I set my heart upon the completion of a liberal education.

The next question to decide was what should be my special work in life. It appeared that in civilization one must have a definite occupation—a profession. I wished to share with my people whatever I might attain, and I looked about me for a distinct field of usefulness apart from the ministry, which was the first to be adopted by the educated Sioux.

Gradually my choice narrowed down to law and medicine, for both of which I had a strong taste; but the latter seemed to me to offer a better opportunity of service to my race; therefore I determined upon the study of medicine long before I entered upon college studies. "Hitch your wagon to a star," says the American philosopher, and this was my star!

College Life in the East

One summer vacation, at my home in Dakota, Dr. Riggs told me the story of Dartmouth College in New Hampshire, and how it was originally founded as a school for Indian youth. The news was timely and good news; and yet I hesitated. I dreaded to cut myself off from my people, and in my heart I knew that if I went, I should not return until I had accomplished my purpose. It was a critical moment in my life, but the decision could be only one way. I taught the little day-school where my first lessons had been learned, throughout the fall term, and in January, 1882, I set out for the far East, at a period when the Government was still at considerable trouble to subdue and settle some of my race upon reservations.

Though a man in years, I had very little practical knowledge of the world, and in my inexperience I was still susceptible to the adventurous and curious side of things rather than to their profounder meanings. Therefore, while somewhat prepared, I was not yet conscious of the seriousness and terrific power of modern civilization.

It was a crisp winter morning when the train pulled into Chicago. . . . It seemed to me that we were being drawn into the deep gulches of the Bad Lands as we entered the city. I realized vividly at that moment that the day of the Indian had passed forever.

I was met at the station by friends, who took me to walk upon some of the main streets. I saw a perfect stream of humanity rushing madly along, and noticed with some surprise that the faces of the people were not happy at all. They wore an intensely serious look that to me was appalling.

I was cautioned against trusting strangers, and told that I must look out for pickpockets. Evidently there were some disadvantages connected with this mighty civilization, for we Indians seldom found it necessary to guard our possessions. It seemed to me that the most dignified men on the streets were the policemen, in their long blue coats with brass buttons. They were such a remarkable set of men physically that this of itself was enough to catch my eye. . . .

After we left Albany, I found myself in a country the like of which, I thought, I would have given much to hunt over before it was stripped of its primeval forests, and while deer and bears roamed over it undisturbed. I looked with delight upon mountains and valleys, and even the little hamlets perched upon the shelves of the high hills. The sight of these rocky farms and little villages reminded me of the presence of an earnest and persistent people. Even the deserted farmhouse, the ruined mill, had an air of saying, "I have done my part in the progress of civilization. Now I can rest." And all the mountains seemed to say, Amen.

What is the great difference between these people and my own? I asked myself. Is it not that the one keeps the old things and continually adds to them new improvements, while the other is too well contented with the old, and will not change his ways nor seek to improve them?

When I reached Boston, I was struck with the old, mossy, granite edifices, and the narrow, crooked streets. Here, too, the people hurried along as if the gray wolf were on their trail. Their ways impressed me as cold, but I forgot that when I had learned to know some of them better.

I went on to Dartmouth College, away up among the granite hills. The country around it is rugged and wild; and thinking of the time when red men lived here in plenty and freedom, it seemed as if I had been destined to come view their graves and bones. No, I said to myself, I have come to continue that which in their last struggle they proposed to take up, in order to save themselves from extinction; but alas! it was too late. Had our New England tribes but followed the example of that great Indian, Samson Occum, and kept up with the development of Dartmouth College, they would have brought forth leaders and men of culture. This was my ambition—that the Sioux should accept civilization before it was too late! I wished that our young men might at once take up the white man's way, and prepare themselves to hold office and wield influence in their native state. Although this hope has not been fully realized, I have the satisfaction of knowing that not a few Indians now hold positions of trust and exercise some political power.

At Dartmouth College I found the buildings much older and more imposing than any I had seen before. There was a true scholastic air about them; in fact, the whole village impressed me as touched with the spirit of learning and refinement. My understanding of English was now so much enlarged as to enable me to grasp current events, as well as the principles of civilization, in a more intelligent manner. . . .

I found Yankees of the uneducated class very Indian-like in their views and habits; a people of strong character, plain-spoken, and opinionated. However, I observed that the students of the academy and their parents were very frugal and saving. Nothing could have been more instructive to me, as we Indians are inclined to be improvident. I had been accustomed to broad, fertile prairies, and liberal ways. Here they seemed to count their barrels of potatoes and apples before they were grown. Every little brooklet was forced to do a river's work in their mills and factories. . . .

Although I had associated with college students for several years, yet I must confess that western college life is quiet compared with that of the tumultuous East. It was here that I had most of my savage gentleness and native refinement knocked out of me. I do not complain, for I know that I gained more than their equivalent. . . .

I was a sort of prodigal son of old Dartmouth, and nothing could have exceeded the heartiness of my welcome. The New England Indians, for whom it was founded, had departed well-nigh a century earlier, and now a warlike Sioux, like a wild fox, had found his way into this splendid seat of learning! Though poor, I was really better off than many of the students, since the old college took care of me under its ancient charter. I was treated with the greatest kindness by the president and faculty, and often encouraged to ask questions and express my own ideas. My uncle's observations in natural history, for which he had a positive genius, the Indian standpoint in sociology and political economy, these were the subject of some protracted discussions in the class room. This became so well understood, that some of my classmates who had failed to prepare their recitations would induce me to take up the time by advancing a native theory or first hand observation.

For the first time, I became really interested in literature and history. Here it was that civilization began to loom up before me colossal in its greatness, when the fact dawned upon me that nations and tongues, as well as individuals, have lived and died. . . . It was under the Old Pine Tree that the Indians were supposed to have met for the last time to smoke the pipe of peace, and under its shadow every graduating. class of my day smoked a parting pipe. . . .

Throughout my student days in the West, I had learned to reverence New England, and especially its metropolis, as the home of culture and art, of morality and Christianity. At that period that sort of thing got a lodging place in my savage mind more readily than the idea of wealth or material power. Somehow I had supposed that Boston must be the home of the nation's elect and not far from the millenium. I was very happy when, after my graduation with the class of 1887, it was made possible for me to study medicine at Boston University. The friends who generously assisted me to realize my great ambition were of the type I had dreamed of, and my home influences in their family all that I could have wished for. A high ideal of duty was placed before me, and I was doubly armed in my original purpose to make my education of service to my race. I continued to study the Christ philosophy and loved it for its essential truths, though doctrines and dogmas often puzzled and repelled me. . . .

Mr. and Mrs. Frank Wood, who were a. father and mother to me at this period of my life, were very considerate of my health and gave me opportunity to enter into many outdoor sports, such as tennis and canoeing, beside regular gymnasium work. . . .

At Dartmouth I had met the English man of letters, Matthew Arnold, and he was kind enough to talk with me for some time. I have also talked with Emerson, Longfellow, Francis Parkman, and many other men of note. Mr. and Mrs. Wood were trustees of Wellesley College and I was so fortunate as to be an occasional visitor there, and to make the acquaintance of Miss Freeman, its first president. I believe the first lecture I ever delivered in public was before the Wellesley girls. I little dreamed that a daughter of mine would ever be among them! . . .

At the seaside hotels, I met society people of an entirely different sort to those I had hitherto taken as American types. I was, I admit, particularly struck with the audacity and forwardness of the women. Among our people the man always leads. I was astonished to learn that some women whom I had observed to accept the most marked attentions from the men were married ladies. Perhaps my earlier training had been too Puritanical, or my aesthetic sense was not then fully developed, for I was surprised when I entered the ballroom to see the pretty women clad so scantily. . . .

At the date of my graduation, in 1890, the Government had fully committed itself to the new and permanent plan of educating the young Indians preparatory to admitting them to citizenship. Various philanthropic societies had been formed expressly to help toward this end. These facts gave weight and momentum to my desire to use all that I had learned for their benefit. I soon received my appointment to the position of Government physician at Pine Ridge agency in South Dakota, to report October first. . . .

A Doctor among the Indians

The Pine Ridge Indian agency was a bleak and desolate looking place in those days, more especially in a November dust storm such as that in which I arrived from Boston to take charge of the medical work of the reservation. In 1890 a "white doctor" who was also an Indian was something of a novelty, and I was afterward informed that there were many and diverse speculations abroad as to my success or failure in this new role, but at the time I was unconscious of an audience. I was thirty-two years of age, but appeared much younger, athletic and vigorous, and alive with energy and enthusiasm.

After reporting to the Indian agent, I was shown to my quarters, which consisted of a bedroom, sitting room, office, and dispensary, all in one continuous barrack with the police quarters and the agent's offices. This barrack was a flimsy one-story affair built of warped cottonwood lumber, and the rude prairie winds whistled musically through the cracks. There was no carpet, no furniture save a plain desk and a couple of hard wooden chairs, and everything was coated with a quarter of an inch or so of fine Dakota dust. This did not disconcert me, however, as I myself was originally Dakota dust! An old-fashioned box stove was the only cheerful thing on the premises, and the first duty I performed was to myself. I built a roaring fire in the stove, and sat down for a few minutes to take a sort of inventory of the situation and my professional prospects.

I had not yet thought seriously of making a life contract with any young woman, and accordingly my place was at the agency mess where the unmarried employees took their meals . . .

It so happened that this was the day of the "Big Issue," on which thousands of Indians scattered over a reservation a hundred miles long by fifty wide, came to the agency for a weekly or fortnightly supply of rations, and it was a veritable "Wild West" array that greeted my astonished eyes. The streets and stores were alive with a motley crowd in picturesque garb, for all wore their best on these occasions. Every road leading to the agency was filled with white-topped lumber wagons, with here and there a more primitive travois, and young men and women on ponies' backs were gaily curveting over the hills. The Sioux belle of that period was arrayed in grass-green or bright purple calico, loaded down with beads and bangles, and sat astride a spotted pony, holding over her glossy uncovered braids and vermilion-tinted cheeks a gaily colored silk parasol.

Toward noon, the whole population moved out two or three miles to a large corral in the midst of a broad prairie, where a herd of beef cattle was held in readiness by the agency cowboys. An Indian with stentorian voice, mounted on a post, announced the names of the group whose steer was to be turned loose. Next moment the flying animal was pursued by two or three swift riders with rifles across their saddles. As the cattle were turned out in quick succession, we soon had a good imitation of the old time buffalo hunt. The galloping, long-horned steers were chased madly in every direction, amid yells and whoops, the firing of guns and clouds of yellow dust, with here and there a puff of smoke and a dull report as one stumbled and fell.

The excitement was soon over, and men of each group were busy skinning the animals, dressing the meat and dividing it among the families interested. Meanwhile the older women, sack in hand, approached the commissary, where they received their regular dole of flour, bacon, coffee, and sugar. Fires were soon blazing merrily in the various temporary camps scattered over the prairie and in the creek bottoms, and after dinner, horse races and dancing were features of the day. Many white sight-seers from adjoining towns were usually on hand. Before night, most of the people had set off in a cloud of dust for their distant homes. . . .

Captain Sword, the dignified and intelligent head of the Indian police force, was very friendly, and soon found time to give me a great deal of information about the place and the people. He said finally:

"*Kola* (my friend), the people are very glad that you have come. You have begun well; we Indians are all your friends. But I fear that we are going to have trouble. I must tell you that a new religion has been proclaimed by some Indians in the Rocky Mountain region, and some time ago, Sitting Bull sent several of his men to investigate. We hear that they have come back, saying that they saw the prophet, or Messiah, who told them that he is God's Son whom He has sent into the world a second time. He told them that He had waited nearly two thousand years for the white men to carry out His teachings, but instead they had destroyed helpless small nations to satisfy their own selfish greed. Therefore He had come again, this time as a Savior to the red people. If they would follow His instructions exactly, in a little while He would cause the earth to shake and destroy all the cities of the white man, when famine and pestilence would come to finish the work. The Indians must live entirely by themselves in their teepees so that the earthquake would not harm them. They must fast and pray and keep up a holy or spirit dance that He taught them. He also ordered them to give up the white man's clothing and make shirts and dresses in the old style.

"My friend," Sword went on, "our reservation has been free from this new teaching until the last few weeks. Quite lately this ghost dance was introduced by Slow Bull and Kicking Bear from Rosebud "—a neighboring agency. "It has been rapidly gaining converts in many of the camps. This is what the council today was about. The agent says that the Great Father at Washington wishes it stopped. I fear the people will not stop. I fear trouble, *Kola*.". . .

I began to think the situation must be serious, and decided to consult some of the educated and Christian Indians. At this juncture a policeman appeared with a note, and handed me my orders, as I supposed. But when I opened it, I read a gracefully worded welcome and invitation to a tea party at the rectory, "to celebrate," the writer said, "my birthday, and your coming to Pine Ridge." I was caught up by the wind of destiny, but at the moment my only thought was of pleasure in the prospect of soon meeting the Reverend Charles Smith Cook, the Episcopal missionary. He was a Yankton Sioux, a graduate of Trinity College and Seabury Divinity School, and I felt sure that I should find in him a congenial friend.

I looked forward to the evening with a peculiar interest. Mr. Cook was delightful, and so was his gracious young wife, who had been a New York girl. . . . Then I met several young ladies, teachers in the boarding school, and a young man or two, and finally Miss Elaine Goodale, who was not entirely a stranger, as I had read her "Apple Blossoms" in Boston, and some of her later articles on Indian education in the *Independent* and elsewhere. Miss Goodale was supervisor of Indian schools in the Dakotas and Nebraska, and she was then at Pine Ridge on a tour of inspection. She was young for such a responsible position, but appeared equal to it in mentality and experience. I thought her very dignified and reserved, but this first evening's acquaintance showed me that she was thoroughly in earnest and absolutely sincere in her work for the Indians. I might as well admit that her personality impressed me deeply. I had laid my plans carefully, and purposed to serve my race for a few years in my profession, after which I would go to some city to practice, and I had decided that it would be wise not to think of marriage for the present. I had not given due weight to the possibility of love.

Events now crowded fast upon one another. It would seem enough that I had at last realized the dream of my life—to be of some service to my people—an ambition implanted by my earlier Indian teachers and fostered by my missionary training. I was really happy in devoting myself mind and body to my hundreds of patients who left me but few leisure moments. . . .

After the second "Big Issue", I had another call from Captain Sword. He began, I believe, by complimenting me upon a very busy day. "Your reputation," he declared, "has already traveled the length and breadth of the reservation. You treat everybody alike, and your directions are understood by the people. No Government doctor has ever gone freely among them before. It is a new order of things. But I fear you have come at a bad time," he added seriously. "The Ghost dancers have not heeded the agent's advice and warning. They pay no attention to us policemen. The craze is spreading like a prairie fire, and the chiefs who are encouraging it do not even come to the agency. They send after their rations and remain at home. It looks bad."

"Do they really mean mischief?" I asked incredulously, for Mr. Cook and I had discussed the matter and agreed in thinking that if the attempt was not made to stop it by force, the craze would die out of itself before long.

"They say not, and that all they ask is to be let alone. They say the white man is not disturbed when he goes to church," Sword replied. "I must tell you, however, that the agent has just ordered the police to call in all Government employees with their families to the agency. This means that something is going to happen. I have heard that he will send for soldiers to come here to stop the Ghost dance. If so, there will be trouble."

As I was still too new to the situation to grasp it fully, I concluded that in any case the only thing for me to do was to apply myself diligently to my special work, and await the issue. . . .

The Ghost Dance War

A religious craze such as that of 1890–91 was a thing foreign to the Indian philosophy. I recalled that a hundred years before, on the overthrow of the Algonquin nations, a somewhat similar faith was evolved by the astute Delaware prophet, brother to Tecumseh. It meant that the last hope of race entity had departed, and my people were groping blindly after spiritual relief in their bewilderment and misery. I believe that the first prophets of the "Red Christ" were innocent enough and that the people generally were sincere, but there were doubtless some who went into it for self-advertisement, and who introduced new and fantastic features to attract the crowd. . . .

I told a visiting government inspector that I still did not believe there was any widespread plot, or deliberate intention to make war upon the whites. In my own mind, I felt sure that the arrival of troops would be construed by the ghost dancers as a threat or a challenge, and would put them at once on the defensive. I was not in favor of that step; neither was Mr. Cook, who was also called into conference; but the officials evidently feared a general uprising, and argued that it was their duty to safeguard the lives of the employees and others by calling for the soldiers without more delay. . . . As a matter of fact, the agent had telegraphed to Fort Robinson for troops before he made a pretense of consulting us Indians, and they were already on their way to Pine Ridge.

I scarcely knew at the time, but gradually learned afterward, that the Sioux had many grievances and causes for profound discontent, which lay back of and were more or less closely related to the ghost dance craze and the prevailing restlessness and excitement. Rations had been cut from time to time; the people were insufficiently fed, and their protests and appeals were disregarded. Never was more ruthless fraud and graft practiced upon a defenseless people than upon these poor natives by the politicians! Never were there more worthless "scraps of paper" anywhere in the world than many of the Indian treaties and Government documents! Sickness was prevalent and the death rate alarming, especially among the children. Trouble from all these causes had for some time been developing, but might have been checked by humane and conciliatory measures. The "Messiah craze" in itself was scarcely a source of danger, and one might almost as well call upon the army to suppress Billy Sunday and his hysterical followers. Other tribes than the Sioux who adopted the new religion were let alone, and the craze died a natural death in the course of a few months. . . .

At this juncture came the startling news from Fort Yates, some two hundred and fifty miles to the north of us, that Sitting Bull had been killed by Indian police while resisting arrest, and a number of his men with him, as well as several of the police. We next heard that the remnant of his band had fled in our direction, and soon afterward, that they had been joined by Big Foot's band from the western part of Cheyenne River agency, which lay directly in their road. United States troops continued to gather at strategic points, and of course the press seized upon the opportunity to enlarge upon the strained situation and predict an "Indian uprising." The reporters were among us, and managed to secure much "news" that no one else ever heard of. Border towns were fortified and cowboys and militia gathered in readiness to protect them against the "red devils." Certain classes of the frontier population industriously fomented the excitement for what there was in it for them, since much money is apt to be spent at such times. As for the poor Indians, they were quite as badly scared as the whites and perhaps with more reason. . . .

During this time of grave anxiety and nervous tension, the cooler heads among us went about our business, and still refused to believe in the tragic possibility of an Indian war. It may be imagined that I was more than busy, though I had not such long distances to cover, for since many Indians accustomed to comfortable log houses were compelled to pass the winter in tents, there was even more sickness than usual. I had access and welcome to the camps of all the various groups and factions. . . .

I had planned to enter upon my life work unhampered by any other ties, and declared that all my love should be vested in my people and my profession. At last, however, I had met a woman whose sincerity was convincing and whose ideals seemed very like my own. . . . She spoke the Sioux language fluently and went among the people with the utmost freedom and confidence. Her methods of work were very simple and direct. I do not know what unseen hand had guided me to her side, but on Christmas day of 1890, Elaine Goodale and I announced our engagement.

Three days later, we learned that Big Foot's band of ghost dancers from the Cheyenne River reservation north of us was approaching the agency, and that Major Whiteside was in command of troops with orders to intercept them.

Late that afternoon, the Seventh Cavalry under Colonel Forsythe was called to the saddle and rode off toward Wounded Knee creek, eighteen miles away. . . .

The morning of December 9th was sunny and pleasant. We were all straining our ears toward Wounded Knee, and about the middle of the forenoon we distinctly heard the reports of the Hotchkiss guns. Two hours later, a rider was seen approaching at full speed, and in a few minutes he had dismounted from his exhausted horse and handed his message to General Brooke's orderly. The Indians were watching their own messenger, who ran on foot along the northern ridges and carried the news to the so-called "hostile" camp. It was said that he delivered his message at almost the same time as the mounted officer.

The resulting confusion and excitement was unmistakable. The white teepees disappeared as if by magic and soon the caravans were in motion, going toward the natural fortress of the "Bad Lands." In the "friendly" camp there was almost as much turmoil, and crowds of frightened women and children poured into the agency. Big Foot's band had been wiped out by the troops, and reprisals were naturally looked for. The enclosure was not barricaded in any way and we had but a small detachment of troops for our protection. Sentinels were placed, and machine guns trained on the various approaches. . . .

On the day following the Wounded Knee massacre there was a blizzard . . .

On the third day it cleared, and the ground was covered with an inch or two of fresh snow. We had feared that some of the Indian wounded might have been left on the field, and a number of us volunteered to go and see. I was placed in charge of the expedition of about a hundred civilians . . . (*a detailed description of the Wounded Knee battlefield and massacre has been deleted.*)

It took all of my nerve to keep my composure in the face of this spectacle, and of the excitement and grief of my Indian companions, nearly every one of whom was crying aloud or singing his death song. The white men became very nervous, but I set them to examining and uncovering every body to see if one were living. Although they had been lying untended in the snow and cold for two days and nights, a number had survived. . . .

All this was a severe ordeal for one who had so lately put all his faith in the Christian love and lofty ideals of the white man. Yet I passed no hasty judgment, and was thankful that I might be of some service and relieve even a small part of the suffering. . . .

In March, all being quiet, Miss Goodale decided to send in her resignation and go East to visit her relatives, and our wedding day was set for the following June.

War with the Politicians

. . . I have tried to make it clear that there was no "Indian outbreak" in 1890–91, and that such trouble as we had may justly be charged to the dishonest politicians, who through unfit appointees first robbed the Indians, then bullied them, and finally in a panic called for troops to suppress them. From my first days at Pine Ridge, certain Indians and white people had taken every occasion to whisper into my reluctant ears the tale of wrongs, real or fancied, committed by responsible officials on the reservation, or by their connivance. To me these stories were unbelievable, from the point of view of common decency. I held that a great government such as ours would never condone or permit any such practices, while administering large trust funds and standing in the relation of guardian to a race made helpless by lack of education and of legal safeguards. At that time, I had not dreamed what American politics really is, and I had the most exalted admiration for our noted public men. Accordingly, I dismissed these reports as mere gossip or the inventions of mischief-makers. . . .

In spite of all that I had gone through, life was not yet a serious matter to me. I had faith in every one, and accepted civilization and Christianity at their face value—a great mistake, as I was to learn later on. I had come back to my people, not to minister to their physical needs alone, but to be a missionary in every sense of the word, and as I was much struck with the loss of manliness and independence in these, the first "reservation Indians" I had ever known, I longed above all things to help them to regain their self-respect.

On June 18, 1891, I was married to Elaine Goodale in the Church of the Ascension, New York City . . .

Our new home was building when we reached Pine Ridge, and we started life together in the old barracks, while planning the finishing and furnishing of the new. . . .

There was nothing I called my own save my dogs and horses and my medicine bags, yet I was perfectly happy, for I had not only gained the confidence of my people, but that of the white residents, and even the border ranchmen called me in now and then. I answered every call, and have ridden forty or fifty miles in a blizzard, over dangerous roads, sometimes at night . . .

(A long section has been deleted in which Ohiyesa obtains personal knowledge of fraud by the Indian agent and his white colleagues against the Sioux and then attempts to support legal proceedings against the Indian agent by the tribe.) I was promptly charged with "insubordination" and other things, but my good friend, General Morgan, then Commissioner, declined to entertain the charges, and I, on my part, kept up the fight at Washington through influential friends, and made every effort to prove my case, or rather, the case of the people, for I had at no time any personal interest in the payment. The local authorities followed the usual tactics, and undertook to force a resignation by making my position at Pine Ridge intolerable. An Indian agent has almost autocratic power, and the conditions of life on an agency are such as to make every resident largely dependent upon his good will. We soon found ourselves hampered in our work and harassed by every imaginable annoyance. My requisitions were overlooked or "forgotten," and it became difficult to secure the necessaries of life. I would receive a curt written order to proceed without delay to some remote point to visit a certain alleged patient; then, before I had covered the distance, would be overtaken

189

by a mounted policeman with arbitrary orders to return at once to the agency. On driving in rapidly and reporting to the agent's office for details of the supposed emergency, I might be rebuked for overdriving the horses, and charged with neglect of some chronic case of which I had either never been informed, or to which it had been physically impossible for me to give regular attention.

. . . the upshot of the affair was that I was shortly offered a transfer. The agent could not be dislodged, and my position had become impossible. The superintendent of the boarding school, a clergyman, and one or two others who had fought on our side were also forced to leave. We had many other warm sympathizers who could not speak out without risking their livelihood.

We declined to accept the compromise, being utterly disillusioned and disgusted with these revelations of Government mismanagement in the field, and realizing the helplessness of the best-equipped Indians to secure a fair deal for their people. Later experience, both my own and that of others, has confirmed me in this view. Had it not been for strong friends in the East and on the press, and the unusual boldness and disregard of personal considerations with which we had conducted the fight, I could not have lasted a month. All other means failing, these men will not hesitate to manufacture evidence against a man's, or a woman's, personal reputation in order to attain their ends.

It was a great disappointment to us both to give up our plans of work and our first home, to which we had devoted much loving thought and most of our little means; but it seemed to us then the only thing to do. We had not the heart to begin the same thing over again elsewhere. I resigned my position in the Indian service, and removed with my family to the city of St. Paul, where I proposed to enter upon the independent practice of medicine.

Civilization as Preached and Practiced

After thirty years of exile from the land of my nativity and the home of my ancestors, I came back to Minnesota in 1893. My mother was born on the shores of Lake Harriet; my great-grandfather's village is now a part of the beautiful park system of the city of Minneapolis. . . .

Although a young couple in a strange city, we were cordially received socially, and while seriously handicapped by lack of means, we had determined to win out. I opened an office, hung out my sign, and waited for patients. It was the hardest work I had ever done! Most of the time we were forced to board for the sake of economy, and were hard put to it to meet office rent and our modest living expenses. . . .

To be sure, I had been bitterly disappointed in the character of the United States army and the honor of Government officials. Still, I had seen the better side of civilization, and I determined that the good men and women who had helped me should not be betrayed. The Christ ideal might be radical, visionary, even impractical, as judged in the light of my later experiences; it still seemed to me logical, and in line with most of my Indian training. My heart was still strong, and I had the continual inspiration of a brave comrade at my side.

With all the rest, I was deeply regretful of the work that I had left behind. I could not help thinking that if the President knew, if the good people of this country knew, of the wrong, it would yet be righted. I had not seen half of the savagery of civilization! While I had plenty of leisure, I began to put upon paper some of my earliest recollections, with the thought that our children might some day like to read of that wilderness life. . . . This was the beginning of my first book, "Indian Boyhood," which was not completed until several years later.

We were slowly gaining ground, when one day a stranger called on me in my office. He was, I learned, one of the field secretaries of the International Committee of Y. M. C. A., and had apparently called to discuss the feasibility of extending this movement among the Indians. *(A section is deleted in which Ohiyesa learns about the programs of the YMCA and then accepts the role as the traveling Indian secretary for the YMCA.)*

. . . I traveled over a large part of the western states and in Canada, visiting the mission stations among Indians of all tribes, and organizing young men's associations wherever conditions permitted. I think I organized some forty-three associations. This gave me a fine opportunity to study Protestant missionary effort among Indians. I seriously considered the racial attitude toward God, and almost unconsciously reopened the book of my early religious training, asking myself how it was that our simple lives were so imbued with the spirit of worship, while much church-going among white and nominally Christian Indians led often to such very small results.

A new point of view came to me then and there. This latter was a machine-made religion. It was supported by money, and more money could only be asked for on the showing made; therefore too many of the workers were after quantity rather than quality of religious experience.

I was constantly meeting with groups of young men of the Sioux, Cheyennes, Crees, Ojibways, and others, in log cabins or little frame chapels, and trying to set before them in simple language the life and character of the Man Jesus. I was cordially received everywhere, and always listened to with the closest attention. Curiously enough, even among these men who were seeking light on the white man's ideals, the racial philosophy emerged from time to time.

I remember one old battle-scarred warrior who sat among the young men got up and said, in substance: "Why, we have followed this law you speak of for untold ages! We owned nothing, because everything is from Him. Food was free, land free as sunshine and rain. Who has changed all this? The white man; and yet he says he is a believer in God! He does not seem to inherit any of the traits of his Father, nor does he follow the example set by his brother Christ."

Another of the older men had attentively followed our Bible study and attended every meeting for a whole week. I finally called upon him for his views. After a long silence, he said:

"I have come to the conclusion that this Jesus was an Indian. He was opposed to material acquirement and to great possessions. He was inclined to peace. He was as unpractical as any Indian and set no price upon his labor of love. These are not the principles upon which the white man has founded his civilization. It is strange that he could not rise to these simple principles which were commonly observed among our people."

These words put the spell of an uncomfortable silence upon our company, but it did not appear that the old man had intended any sarcasm or unkindness, for after a minute he added that he was glad we had selected such an unusual character for our model. . . .

My two uncles who were in the Custer fight lived in Canada from the time of our flight in 1862, and both died there. I was happy to be sent to that part of the country in time to see the elder one alive. He had been a father to me up to the age of fifteen, and I had not seen him for over twenty years. I found him a farmer, living in a Christian community. I had sent word in advance of my coming, and my uncle's family had made of it a great occasion. All of my old playmates were there. My uncle was so happy that tears welled up in his eyes. "When we are old," he smiled, "our hearts are not strong in moments like this. The Great Spirit has been kind to let me see my boy again before I die." The early days were recalled as we feasted together, and all agreed that the chances were I should have been killed before reaching the age of twenty, if I had remained among them; for, said they, I was very anxious to emulate my uncle, who had been a warrior of great reputation. Afterward I visited the grave of my grandmother, whose devotion had meant so much to me as a motherless child. This was one of the great moments of my life.

Throughout this period of my work I was happy, being unhampered by official red tape in the effort to improve conditions among my people. . . .

Among other duties of my position, I was expected to make occasional speaking trips through the East to arouse interest in the work, and it thus happened that I addressed large audiences in Chicago, New York, Boston, and at Lake Mohonk. I was taken by slum and settlement workers to visit the slums and dives of the cities, which gave another shock to my ideals of "Christian civilization." Of course, I had seen something of the poorer parts of Boston during my medical course, but not at night, and not in a way to realize the horror and wretchedness of it as I did now. To be sure, I had been taught even as a child that there are always some evil minded men in every nation, and we knew well what it is to endure physical hardship, but our poor lost nothing of their self-respect and dignity. Our great men not only divided their last kettle of food with a neighbor, but if great grief should come to them, such as the death of child or wife, they would voluntarily give away their few possessions and begin life over again in token of their sorrow. We could not conceive of the extremes of luxury and misery existing thus side by side, for it was common observation with us that the coarse weeds, if permitted to grow, will choke out the more delicate flowers. These things troubled me very much; yet I still held before my race the highest, and as yet unattained, ideals of the white man. . . .

My effort was to make the Indian feel that Christianity is not at fault for the white man's sins, but rather the lack of it, and I freely admitted that this nation is not Christian, but declared that the Christians in it are trying to make it so. I found the facts and the logic of them often hard to dispute, but was partly consoled by the wonderful opportunity to come into close contact with the racial mind, and to refresh my understanding of the philosophy in which I had been trained, but which had been overlaid and superseded by a college education. I do not know how much good I accomplished, but I did my best.

At the Nation's Capital

My work for the International Committee of the Y.M.C.A. brought me into close association with some of the best products of American civilization. . . . Had I not known some such, I should long ago have gone back to the woods.

I wished very much to resume my profession of medicine, but I was as far as ever from having the capital for a start, and we had now three children. At this juncture, I was confronted by what seemed a hopeful opportunity. Some of the leading men of the Sioux, among them my own brother, Rev. John Eastman, came to me for a consultation. They argued that I was the man of their tribe best fitted to look after their interests at Washington. . . .Although not a lawyer, they gave me power of attorney to act for them in behalf of these claims, and to appear as their representative before the Indian Bureau, the President, and Congress.

After signing the necessary papers, I went to Washington, where I urged our rights throughout two sessions and most of a third, while during the summers I still traveled among the Sioux. I learned that scarcely one of our treaties with the United States had been carried out in good faith in all of its provisions. . . . *(A long section is deleted in which Ohiyesa enumerates many injustices of the US government against many different Indian tribes.)*

Now for the first time I seriously studied the machinery of government, and before I knew it, I was a lobbyist. I came to Washington with a great respect for our public men and institutions. Although I had had some disillusioning experiences with the lower type of political henchmen on the reservations, I reasoned that it was because they were almost beyond the pale of civilization and clothed with supreme authority over a helpless and ignorant people, that they dared do the things they did. Under the very eye of the law and of society, I thought, this could scarcely be tolerated. I was confident that a fair hearing would be granted, and our wrongs corrected without undue delay. I had overmuch faith in the civilized ideal, and I was again disappointed. . . .

The officials received me courteously enough, and assured me that the matters I spoke of should be attended to, but as soon as my back was turned, they pigeonholed them. After waiting patiently, I would resort to the plan of getting one of the Massachusetts Senators, who were my friends, to ask for the papers in the case, and this was generally effective. . . .

I would approach a legislator who was a stranger to me, in the hope of being allowed to explain to him the purport of our measure. He would listen a while and perhaps refer me to some one else. I would call on the man he named, and to my disgust be met with a demand for a liberal percentage on the whole amount to be recovered. If I refused to listen to this proposal, I would soon find the legislator in question "drumming up" some objection to the bill, and these tactics would be kept up until we yielded, or made some sort of compromise. . . .

As I have said, nearly every Indian delegation that came to the capital in those days—and they were many—appealed to me for advice, and often had me go over their business with them before presenting it. . . . The old men often amused me by their shrewd comments upon our public men. . . .

An old chief said of President McKinley: "I never knew a white man show so much love for mother and wife." "He has a bigger heart than most white men," declared Little-fish, "and this is unfortunate for him. The white man is a man of business, and has no use for a heart."

One day, I found a number of the chiefs in the Senate gallery. They observed closely the faces and bearing of the legislators and then gave their verdict. One man they compared to a fish. Another had not the attitude of a true man; that is, he held to a pose. Senator Morgan of Alabama they called a great councilor. Senator Hoar they estimated as a patriotic and just statesman. They picked out Senator Platt of Connecticut as being very cautious and a diplomat. They had much difficulty in judging Senator Tillman, but on the whole they considered him to be a fighting man, governed by his emotions rather than his judgment. . . . Senator Turpie of Indiana they took for a preacher, and were pleased with his air of godliness and reverence. Senator Frye of Maine they thought must be a rarity among white men—honest to the core! . . .

Theodore Roosevelt has been well known to the Sioux for over twenty-five years, dating from the years of his ranch life. He was well liked by them as a rule. Spotted Horse said of him, "While he talked, I forgot that he was a white man.". . .

I have been much interested in the point of view of these older Indians. Our younger element has now been so thoroughly drilled in the motives and methods of the white man, at the same time losing the old mother and family training through being placed in boarding school from six years of age onward, that they have really become an entirely different race. . . .

Back to the Woods

In the summer of 1910, I accepted a commission to search out and purchase rare curios and ethnological specimens for one of the most important collections in the country. Very few genuine antiques are now to be found among Indians living on reservations, and the wilder and more scattered bands who still treasure them cannot easily be induced to give them up. My method was one of indirection. I would visit for several days in a camp where I knew, or had reason to believe, that some of the coveted articles were to be found. After I had talked much with the leading men, feasted them, and made them presents, a slight hint would often result in the chief or medicine man "presenting" me with some object of historic or ceremonial interest, which etiquette would not permit to be "sold," and which a white man would probably not have been allowed to see at all.

Within the zone of railroads and automobiles there is, I believe, only one region left in which a few roving bands of North American Indians still hold civilization at bay. The great inland seas of northern Minnesota and the Province of Ontario are surrounded by almost impenetrable jungle, the immense bogs called "muskeggs" filled with tamaracks, and the higher land with Norway, white and "jack" pines, white and red cedar, poplar and birch. The land is a paradise for moose, deer and bears, as well as the smaller fur-bearers, and the glistening black waters are a congenial home for north-ern fish of all kinds, of which the sturgeon is king. The water-fowl breed there in countless numbers. There are blueberries and cranberries in abundance, while the staple cereal of that region, the full-flavored wild rice, is found in the inland bays by thousands of acres.

Of this miniature world of freedom and plenty a few northern Ojibways, a branch of the great Algonquin race, are the present inhabitants, living quite to themselves and almost unconscious of the bare pathos of their survival. . . . Fortunately or unfortunately, the labyrinth in which they dwell has thus far protected them far more effectually than any treaty rights could possibly do from his (*the white man's*) almost indecent enterprise.

I know of no Indians within the borders of the United States, except those of Leech, Cass and Red Lakes in Minnesota, who still sustain themselves after the old fashion by hunting, fishing and the gathering of wild rice and berries. They do, to be sure, have a trifle of annuity money from the sale of their pine lands, and now and then they sell a few trinkets. Their permanent houses are of logs or frame, but they really do not live in them except during the coldest part of the year. Even then, some of them may be found far away from their villages, trapping for furs, which may still be disposed of at convenient points along the Canadian border. They travel by canoe or on foot, as they own very few horses, and there are no roads through the forest—only narrow trails, deeply grooved in the virgin soil.

The Leech Lake Ojibways, to whom I made my first visit, appear perfectly contented and irresponsible. They have plenty to eat of the choicest wild game, wild rice and berries. The making of maple sugar is a leading industry. The largest band and by far the most interesting is that which inhabits Bear Island, plants no gardens, will have nothing to do with schools or churches, and meets annually, as of old, for the "Grand Medicine Dance," or sacred festival, invoking the protection and blessing of the "Great Mystery" for the year to come.

I am a Sioux, and the Ojibways were once the fiercest of our enemies, yet I was kindly welcomed by the principal chief, Majigabo, who even permitted me to witness the old rites upon their "sacred ground." This particular spot, they told me, had been in use for more than forty years, and the moose-hide drum, stretched upon a cylinder of bass-wood, was fully as venerable. The dance-hall was about a hundred feet long, roofed with poles and thatch. In the center was a rude altar, and the entrance faced the rising sun. . . .

Majigabo is one of the few Indians left alive who has ventured to defy a great government with a handful of savages. Only a few years ago, Captain Wilkinson was shot down at the head of his troop, while advancing to frighten the Bear Islanders into obedience. The trouble originated in the illegal sale of whisky to the Indians. One of the tribesmen was summoned to Duluth as a witness, and at the close of the trial turned loose to walk home, a distance of over a hundred miles. The weather was severe and he reached his people half-starved and sick from exposure, and the next time one was summoned, he not unnaturally refused to appear. After the death of Captain Wilkinson, no further attempt was made at coercion.

"They can take everything else, but they must let me and these island people alone," the chief said to me, and I could not but sympathize with his attitude. Only last spring he refused to allow the census taker to enumerate his people. . . .

These aboriginal woodsmen are in type quite distinct from the Plains Indians. They are generally tall and well-proportioned, of somewhat lighter complexion than their brethren to the southward, and very grave and reticent. Their homes and food are practically those of two centuries ago, the only change observable being that the inconvenient blanket is for the most part discarded and the men carry guns instead of bows and arrows. . . .

At North Bay I heard of a remarkable old woman, said to be well over ninety years of age, the daughter of a long-time chief during the good old days. I called at her solitary birch-bark teepee, and found her out, but she soon returned bent under a load of bark for making mats, with roots and willow twigs for dye. She was persuaded to sit for her picture and even to tell some old stories of her people, which she did with much vivacity. There are less than a hundred of them left!

The Soul of the White Man

My last work under the auspices of the Government was the revision of the Sioux allotment rolls, including the determination of family groups, and the assignment of surnames when these were lacking. . . . This work occupied me for six years, and gave me insight into the relationships and intimate history of thirty thousand Sioux.

My first book, *Indian Boyhood*, embodying the recollections of my wild life, appeared in 1902, and the favor with which it was received has encouraged me to attempt a fuller expression of our people's life from the inside. The present is the eighth that I have done, always with the devoted cooperation of my wife. . . .

None of my earlier friends who knew me well would ever have believed that I was destined to appear in the role of a public speaker! It may be that I shared the native gift of oratory in some degree, but I had also the Indian reticence with strangers. . . .

My chief object has been, not to entertain, but to present the American Indian in his true character before Americans. The barbarous and atrocious character commonly attributed to him has dated from the transition period, when the strong drink, powerful temptations, and commercialism of the white man led to deep demoralization. Really it was a campaign of education on the Indian and his true place in American history.

I have been, on the whole, happily surprised to meet with so cordial a response. Again and again I have been told by recognized thinkers, "You present an entirely new viewpoint. We can never again think of the Indian as we have done before." A great psychologist wrote me after reading "The Soul of the Indian": "My God! why did we not know these things sooner?" Many of my hearers have admitted that morality and spirituality are found to thrive better under the simplest conditions than in a highly organized society, and that the virtues are more readily cultivated where the "struggle for existence" is merely a struggle with the forces of nature, and not with one's fellow-men.

The philosophy of the original American was demonstrably on a high plane, his gift of eloquence, wit, humor and poetry is well established; his democracy and community life was much nearer the ideal than ours to-day; his standard of honor and friendship unsurpassed, and all his faults are the faults of generous youth.

It was not until I felt that I had to a degree established these claims, that I consented to appear on the platform in our ancestral garb of honor. I feel that I was a pioneer in this new line of defense of the native American, not so much of his rights in the land as of his character and religion. I am glad that the drift is now toward a better understanding, and that he is become the acknowledged hero of the Boy Scouts and Camp Fire Girls, as well as of many artists, sculptors, and sincere writers.

I was invited to represent the North American Indian at the First Universal Races Congress in London, England, in 1911. It was a great privilege to attend that gathering of distinguished representatives of 53 different nationalities, come together to mutually acquaint themselves with one another's progress and racial ideals. I was entertained by some well known men, but there was little time for purely social enjoyment. What impressed me most was the perfect equality of the races, which formed the background of all the discussions. It was declared at the outset that there is no superior race, and no inferior, since individuals of all races have proved their innate capacity by their standing in the universities of the world, and it has not seldom happened that men of the undeveloped races have surpassed students of the most advanced races in scholarship and ability. . . .

It has been my privilege to visit nearly all sections of our country on lecture tours, including semi-tropical Florida and the Pacific coast, the great prairie states, and almost every nook and corner of picturesque New England. I have been entertained at most of our great colleges and universities, from coast to coast, and had the honor of acquaintance with many famous and interesting people, . . .

From the time I first accepted the Christ ideal it has grown upon me steadily, but I also see more and more plainly our modern divergence from that ideal. I confess I have wondered much that Christianity is not practiced by the very people who vouch for that wonderful conception of exemplary living. It appears that they are anxious to pass on their religion to all races of men, but keep very little of it themselves. I have not yet seen the meek inherit the earth, or the peacemakers receive high honor.

Why do we find so much evil and wickedness practiced by the nations composed of professedly "Christian" individuals? The pages of history are full of licensed murder and the plundering of weaker and less developed peoples, and obviously the world today has not outgrown this system. Behind the material and intellectual splendor of our civilization, primitive savagery and cruelty and lust hold sway, undiminished, and as it seems, unheeded. When I let go of my simple, instinctive nature religion, I hoped to gain something far loftier as well as more satisfying to the reason. Alas! it is also more confusing and contradictory. The higher and spiritual life, though first in theory, is clearly secondary, if not entirely neglected, in actual practice. When I reduce civilization to its lowest terms, it becomes a system of life based upon trade. The dollar is the measure of value, and *might* still spells *right;* otherwise, why war?

Yet even in deep jungles God's own sunlight penetrates, and I stand before my own people still as an advocate of civilization. Why? First, because there is no chance for our former simple life any more; and second, because I realize that the white man's religion is not responsible for his mistakes. There is every evidence that God has given him all the light necessary by which to live in peace and good-will with his brother; and we also know that many brilliant civilizations have collapsed in physical and moral decadence. It is for us to avoid their fate if we can.

I am an Indian; and while I have learned much from civilization, for which I am grateful, I have never lost my Indian sense of right and justice. I am for development and progress along social and spiritual lines, rather than those of commerce, nationalism, or material efficiency. Nevertheless, so long as I live, I am an American.

Bibliography of Works
by Charles Eastman (*Ohiyesa*)

Indian Boyhood
—New York: McClure, Philips & Co., 1902
—Garden City, N.Y.: Doubleday, Page & Co., 1915
—Boston: Little, Brown, & Co. [1924]
—Greenwich, N.Y.: Fawcett Publications Ltd, 1970
—New York: Dover Publications, 1971
—Glorieta, N.M.: Rio Grande Press, [1976]
—Lincoln: University of Nebraska Press, 1991
—Alexandria, Va.: Time-Life Books, 1993

Red Hunters and the Animal People
—New York and London: Harper & Brothers, 1904
—New York: AMS Press, 1976

Old Indian Days
—New York: The McClure Company, 1907
—Boston: Little, Brown, & Co. [1924]
—Lincoln: University of Nebraska Press, [1991]

Wigwam Evenings: Sioux Folk Tales (with Elaine Goodale Eastman)
—Boston: Little, Brown, & Co. [1909]
—Lincoln: University of Nebraska Press, [1990]
—Mineola, N.Y.: Dover Publications, 2000

Smoky Day's Wigwam Evenings; Indian stories Retold
—Boston: Little, Brown, & Co, 1910

The Soul of the Indian: An Interpretation
—Boston: Houghton Mifflin Co., 1911
—New York: Johnson Reprint Corp., 1971

—Lincoln: University of Nebraska Press, 1980
—San Rafael, C.A.: New World Library, 1993
—Mamaroneck, N.Y.: Aeon Pub. Co., 2000
—New York: Dover Publications, 2003

Indian Child Life
—Boston: Little, Brown, and Co., 1913

Indian Scout Talks: A Guide for Boy Scouts and Campfire Girls
—Boston: Little, Brown, & Co., 1914
—New York: Dover [1974]

The Indian Today: The Past and Future of the first American
—Garden City, N.Y.: Doubleday, Page & Co., 1915
—New York: AMS Press, 1975

From Deep Woods Into Civilization: Chapters in the Autobiography of an Indian
—Boston: Little, Brown, & Co., 1916, 1920, 1925
—Lincoln: University of Nebraska Press, 1977
—Chicago: R. Donnelley & Sons Co., 2001
—Mineola, N.Y.: Dover Publications, 2003

Indian Heroes and Great Chieftains
—Boston: Little, Brown, & Co., 1918
—Lincoln: University of Nebraska Press, [1991]
—Mineola, N.Y.: Dover, 1997

Biographical Notes

About Ohiyesa

OHIYESA (CHARLES ALEXANDER EASTMAN) was born in a buffalo hide tipi near Redwood Falls, Minn., in the winter of 1858. His father, "Many Lightnings" (Tawakanhdeota), was a full-blood Sioux. His mother was the granddaughter of the Sioux Chief "Cloud Man" and the daughter of Stands Sacred (Wakan inajin win) and a well-known army officer, Seth Eastman. His name at birth was "Hakadah," the pitiful last, because he became the last of his three brothers and one sister when his mother died shortly after his birth. In his early youth he received the name Ohiyesa (The Winner).

The baby was initially raised in his homeland of Minnesota by his grandmother. At the age of four, the so-called "Sioux Uprising of 1862" occurred and he became separated from his father, elder brothers and only sister, whom the tribe thought had been killed by the whites. Hakadah fled into exile in Manitoba with the remaining members of his band of Santee Sioux. For the next eleven years he lived the original nomadic life of his people in the care of his uncle and his grandmother. His uncle was a prominent hunter and warrior and gave the youth, now named Ohiyesa, the complete training necessary to carry on the nomadic tribal heritage, including all of the secrets of virgin nature. Both his uncle and grandmother instilled in him the spiritual philosophy of the Indian. Ohiyesa always regarded this period of his life as his most important education.

At fifteen, Ohiyesa had just entered Indian manhood and was preparing to embark on his first war-path to avenge the reputed death of his father, when he was astonished by the reappearance of his father. The young man learned that this father had adopted the religion and customs of the hated race, and was come to take home his youngest son.

His father was part of a small group of progressive Indians who earned a living with a combination of farming and ranching on homesteads in Flandreau, Dakota Territory. After Ohiyesa's first experience with a mission day school, he contemplated rebelling and leaving his new log home to return to the wild and his native ways. However after a long discussion with his father, he cut his long hair, began to wear white man's clothing and applied himself to his new school life. He soon overcame his reluctance, although not his unhappiness with his new world, and two years later walked 150 miles to attend a better school at Santee, Nebraska. In this larger school he made rapid progress and upon the recommendation of his teacher, the renowned missionary educator, Dr. Alfred L. Riggs, Ohiyesa was accepted at to the preparatory department of Beloit College, Wisconsin. His father had adopted the English name of his wife's father, Eastman, so the boy now named himself Charles Alexander Eastman.

Ohiyesa, now primarily known as Charles Eastman, spent two years at Beloit College before successively going to Knox College, Ill.; then Kimball Union Academy in New Hampshire, and finally to Dartmouth College. He graduated from Dartmouth in 1887, and then studied medicine at Boston University, where he graduated in 1890 as orator of his class. He spent a total of seventeen years in primary, preparatory, undergraduate college, and professional education, which is significantly less time than is required by a typical student.

During his studies in the East he made the acquaintance of many prominent people who would later help him further his career. With their help his first position was as Government Physician for the Sioux at the Pine Ridge reservation in South Dakota. He was at Pine Ridge before, during and after the "Ghost dance" rebellion of 1890-91, and he cared for the wounded Indians after the massacre at Wounded Knee. In 1891 he married a white woman who was also working at the Pine Ridge reservation, Miss Elaine Goodale of Berkshire County, Mass. Shortly after returning from his wedding in the East, the corrupt Indian agent forced Eastman to resign his job at the agency in retaliation for Eastman's attempt to help the Sioux prove crimes against the agent and the agent's white friends. In 1893 he, his wife and their new baby moved to St. Paul, Minnesota, where he started a medical practice. Shortly thereafter he accepted a position as field secretary for the International Committee of the YMCA, and for three years traveled extensively throughout the United States and Canada visiting many Indian tribes in an attempt to start new YMCA's in those areas.

In 1897 Dr. Eastman went to Washington as the legal representative and lobbyist for the Sioux tribe. From 1899 to 1902 he again served as a Government physician to the Sioux at Crow Creek Agency, South Dakota. Starting in 1903, as an employee of the Indian Bureau, he spent over six years giving permanent English family names to the Sioux. In the process of creating both English names and family lineage records he met and interviewed almost every living member of the Sioux tribe.

His first book, "Indian Boyhood," was published in 1902. It is the story of his own early life in the wilds of Canada, and it was an immediate public success generating public notoriety and a demand for more of his writings. He wrote a total of eleven books, including *Red Hunters and the Animal People* (1904), *Old Indian Days* (1906), *Wigwam Evenings* (1909), *Smoky Day's Wigwam Evenings: Indian Stories Retold* (1910), *The Soul of the Indian* (1911), *Indian Child Life* (1913), *Indian Scout Talks* (1914), *The Indian Today: The Past and Future of the First American* (1915), *From the Deep Woods to Civilization* (1916) *Indian Heroes and Great Chieftains* (1918). All of his books were successful, some were used in school editions, and many were translated into French, German, Danish, and Czech languages. He also contributed numerous articles to magazines, reviews, and encyclopedias.

In 1910 Eastman began his long association with the Boy Scouts, helping Ernest Thompson Seton establish the organization based in large part on the prototype of the American Indian. It was also at about this time that he started to become in high demand as a lecturer and public speaker, traveling extensively in the US and abroad. Eastman was chosen to represent the American Indian at the Universal Races Congress in London in 1911. His public speaking continued for the remainder of his life.

Beginning in 1910 and for the rest of his life, Eastman also became involved with many progressive organizations attempting to improve the circumstances of the various Indian tribes. At one time he was president of the Society of American Indians, one prominent organization of that type.

From 1915 to 1920 the Eastman family created and operated a summer camp for girls, Oahe, at Granite Lake, New Hampshire, attempting to teach Indian life-ways to young girls.

He and his wife separated in August 1921. While the couple declined to comment on the reason for their separation, descendants later commented that they believed that the primary reason was the increasing dispute between the couple regarding the best future for the American Indian. Elaine Goodale Eastman stressed total assimilation of Native Americans into the dominant society and she apparently increasingly tried to dominate her husband's views.[1] Eastman favored a type of cultural pluralism in which Indians would interact with the dominant society, utilizing only those positive aspects that would benefit them, but still retaining their Indian identity, including their traditional beliefs and customs; in effect living between two worlds. Eastman believed

---

1. The interviews on which these conclusions are based are set forth in detail in the most authoritative biography on his life: Wilson, Raymond, *Ohiyesa: Charles Eastman, Santee Sioux*, University of Illinois Press, Urbana, 1983.

that the teachings and spirit of his adopted religion of Christianity and the traditional Indian spiritual beliefs were essentially the same and had their common origins in the same "Great Mystery;" a belief that was controversial to many Christians.

In 1928 Eastman purchased land on the north shore of Lake Huron, near Desbarats, Ontario, Canada. For the remainder of his life, when he was not traveling and lecturing, he lived there in his primitive cabin in communion with the virgin nature that he loved so dearly. In his last years he spent only the coldest winter months with his son in Detroit, where he died on January 8, 1939, at the age of eighty. For several years toward the end of his life he worked on a major study on the Sioux, but the project was never completed.

As stated in the preface, in his later adult life he was the foremost Indian spokesman of his day and his contribution to our understanding of the American Indian philosophy and religion are so significant that at the 1933 Chicago World's Fair, Eastman was presented a special medal honoring the most distinguished achievements by an American Indian.

About Michael Oren Fitzgerald

MICHAEL OREN FITZGERALD has written and edited numerous publications on world religions, predominantly on American Indian spirituality. Four of his books on American Indian spirituality are used in college courses. Three of the books Fitzgerald has co-edited with his wife, Judith Fitzgerald, have received prestigious awards, including Best Book on Religion and Philosophy – 2005 by the Midwest Independent Publisher's Association for *The Spirit of Indian Women.* He holds a Doctor of Jurisprudence, cum laude, from Indiana University. Michael has taught Religious Traditions of North American Indians in the Indiana University Continuing Studies Department in Bloomington, Indiana. Fitzgerald has spent extended periods of time visiting traditional cultures and attending sacred ceremonies throughout the world, including the sacred rites of the Apsaroke, Sioux, Cheyenne, Shoshone, Bannock, and Apache tribes. He is an adopted son of the late Thomas Yellowtail, one of the most honored American Indian spiritual leaders of the last century, who also adopted Fitzgerald into the Crow tribe in 1971. He and his wife have an adult son and live in Bloomington, Indiana.

> "My son, Michael Fitzgerald, has benn a member of my family and the Crow tribe for over twenty years. Michael has helped to preserve the spiritual tradition of the Crow Sun Dance and he has helped to show us the wisdom of the old-timers."
> —Thomas Yellowtail, Crow Medicine Man and Sun Dance Chief

> "Michael Fitzgerald has heard the poignant narratives of the American Indian people, and has lived among the Crow people for extended periods of time since 1970. We thank Fitzgerald for his deep-seated appreciation, honor and respect for American Indian culture, its religion, language and lifeways."
> —Janine Pease, founding president of the Little Big Horn College, and recipient of the National Indian Educator of the Year Award

About Janine Pease

DR. JANINE PEASE is the founding president of the Little Big Horn College in Crow Agency Montana, a past president of the American Indian Higher Education Consortium (for two terms), a director of the American Indian College Fund (for seven years), and was appointed by President Clinton to the National Advisory Council on Indian Education (for eight years). She holds a B.A. from Central Washington University and a Doctorate of Education from Montana State University. Janine has won several prestigious awards: National Indian Educator of the Year (1990), The MacArthur Fellowship Award (better known as the "Genius Award") and the ACLU Jeanette Rankin Award. She has been named one of the "One Hundred Montanan's of the Century" by the Missoulian Magazine, a "Montanans To Remember" by Montana Magazine, and one of the 14 most important American Indians leaders of the 20th century in *New Warriors,* by R. David Edmunds (University of Nebraska Press). She is also the recipient of Honorary Doctorate degrees from six different colleges and universities. Janine is a Crow and Hidatsa Indian, enrolled as a Crow. She has two adult children and lives in Lodge Grass, Montana.

About Raymond Wilson

RAYMOND WILSON is the chairman of the History Department at Fort Hays State University in Kansas. He is a past recipient of the Kansas "Governor's Medal of Merit". His numerous books include *Native Americans in the Twentieth Century* and *Indian Lives: Essays on Nineteenth and Twentieth Century Native American Leaders.* His book *Ohiyesa: Charles Eastman, Santee Sioux* is the most comprehensive biography ever written on the life of Charles Eastman (Ohiyesa). He has one adult son and he and his wife live in Hays, Kansas.

Index

For a glossary of all key foreign words used in books published by World Wisdom, including metaphysical terms in English, consult: www.DictionaryofSpiritualTerms.org.
This on-line Dictionary of Spiritual Terms provides extensive definitions, examples and related terms in other languages.

Other Books by Michael Oren Fitzgerald

Yellowtail: Crow Medicine Man and Sun Dance Chief,
University of Oklahoma Press, 1991

*Light on the Indian World: The Essential Writings
of Charles Eastman (Ohiyesa),* by Charles Eastman
edited by Michael O. Fitzgerald, World Wisdom, 2002

The Foundations of Christian Art: Illustrated, by Titus Burckhardt,
edited by Michael Oren Fitzgerald, World Wisdom, 2006

*The Spiritual Legacy of the American Indian: Commemorative Edition
with Letters While Living with Black Elk,* by Joseph Epes Brown,
co-edited by Michael Oren Fitzgerald, World Wisdom, 2007

Native Spirit: The Sun Dance Way, by Thomas Yellowtail,
edited by Michael Oren Fitzgerald, World Wisdom, 2007

*Introduction to Hindu Dharma: Discourses by
the 68th Jagadguru of Kanchi,*
edited by Michael Oren Fitzgerald, World Wisdom, 2008

Other Books by Judith Fitzgerald and Michael Oren Fitzgerald

Christian Spirit, World Wisdom, 2004
{Awarded best book on "Religion and Philosophy"—2004 by *MIPA*}

Indian Spirit: Revised and Enlarged, World Wisdom, 2006

The Sermon of All Creation: Christians on Nature, World Wisdom, 2005
{Merit Award Winner for "Religion and Philosophy" —2005 by *MIPA*}
{Merit Award Winner for "Nature"—2005 by *MIPA*}

The Spirit of Indian Women, World Wisdom, 2005
{Awarded best book on "Religion and Philosophy"—2005 by *MIPA*}
{Awarded best book on "Multi-Cultural"—2005 by *MIPA*}

The Universal Spirit of Islam, World Wisdom, 2006

The Spirit of Muhammad: From Hadith, World Wisdom, 2008

Films Produced by Michael Oren Fitzgerald

Native Spirit & The Sun Dance Way, World Wisdom, 2007
{Offical Selection— Montreal *First Peoples Festival*}
{Offical Selection—31st Annual *American Indian Film Festival*}

Other American Indian Books and Films by World Wisdom

All Our Relatives: Traditional Native American Thoughts about Nature,
compiled and illustrated by Paul Goble, 2005

The Essential Charles Eastman (Ohiyesa): Light on the Indian World,
by Charles Eastman (Ohiyesa),
edited by Michael Oren Fitzgerald, 2007

The Feathered Sun: Plains Indians in Art and Philosophy
by Frithjof Schuon, 1990

The Gospel of the Redman: Commemorative Edition,
compiled by Ernest Thompson Seton and Julia M. Seton, 2005

Indian Spirit: Revised and Enlarged,
edited by Judith Fitzgerald and Michael Oren Fitzgerald, 2006

Native Spirit: The Sun Dance Way, by Thomas Yellowtail,
edited by Michael Oren Fitzgerald, World Wisdom, 2007

Native Spirit & The Sun Dance Way, directed by Jennifer Casey,
produced by Michael Oren Fitzgerlad, World Wisdom, 2007

The Spirit of Indian Women, edited by Judith Fitzgerald and
Michael Oren Fitzgerald, 2005

*The Spiritual Legacy of the American Indian: Commemorative Edition
with Letters While Living with Black Elk,* by Joseph Epes Brown,
co-edited by Michael Oren Fitzgerald, 2007

Tipi: Home of the Nomadic Buffalo Hunters,
by Paul Goble, 2007